PRAISE FOR
The Sacred Path of the Soulmate

"An illuminating, eloquent, soul-spanning treatise
on love. Gerald Sze's immaculate storytelling
opens our hearts and minds by tying up the
loose ends to the age-old questions of why we
love who we love when we love."

ZHENA MUZYKA, author of *Life by the Cup*

"Gerald Sze elegantly gives romantic love its
rightful place in spirituality. This book has the
power to transform the reader and the reader's
relationships. Altogether beautiful."

SYNTHIA ANDREWS, ND, author of *The Path of Energy*

"The consumerist approach to love focuses
on attracting the "right person" to fulfill one's
shopping list of desires. Gerald Sze counters
this with the refreshing view that love is a lifelong
opportunity to better ourselves. This book
has the potential to become a platform
for a renewal of true love."

FRANK RA, author of *Exstatica*

GERALD SZE

THE
SACRED
PATH
OF THE
SOULMATE

Embracing
True Romantic Love

Published by
LifeTree Media Ltd.
www.lifetreemedia.com

Distributed by
Greystone Books Ltd.
www.greystonebooks.com

Page 229 constitutes a continuation of the copyright page.

Cataloguing data available from Library and Archives Canada
ISBN 978-1-928055-26-6 (paperback)
ISBN 978-1-928055-27-3 (EPUB)
ISBN 978-1-928055-28-0 (PDF)

Editing by Maggie Langrick and Lynne Melcombe
Copyediting by Gillian Burnett
Cover design by Peter Cocking
Interior design by Naomi MacDougall
Printed and bound in Canada
Distributed in the U.S. by Publishers Group West

EDITOR'S NOTE: The lack of a singular gender-neutral pronoun in the English language has stymied the clear and inclusive written expression of many progressive thinkers. In this book, you will see the use of "they" and "them" to refer to singular subjects whose gender is unknown or inconsequential, as is often the case in English spoken aloud. This is an intentional editorial decision driven by the desire to be inclusive toward readers of all genders and orientations. Where the author uses gendered pronouns, it is because he is referring to specific individuals whose gender identity aligns with the pronoun used.

*This book is dedicated to my
two sisters, and to all the romantic
lovers who have the courage
to seek true love.*

CONTENTS

ACKNOWLEDGMENTS

I WOULD LIKE to thank my publisher and lead editor, Maggie Langrick, for believing in this project and in me. Maggie's vision, compassion and thoughtful care have steered the direction of this book, bringing new life to the manuscript and the book's title. I am privileged to be in her world, and to be part of the LifeTree family.

I also thank my editor, Lynne Melcombe, for being the midwife of this book, shepherding me through the process every step of the way. She has enlivened this book with her personal life experiences and intellectual insights, and it would not be the same without her dedication and creativity.

I am also grateful to copyeditor Gillian Burnett for stepping in when the manuscript needed an objective mind to further strengthen and clarify the text.

Thank you to the LifeTree Media publishing team for seeing this book through to its final form. Specific thanks to Paris Spence-Lang for his super organizing skill and patience. Without him, the process would not have been so seamless or as much fun.

Great thanks also go out to my family and friends. Ryan Aceman edited the original version of the manuscript front to back, to make the raw manuscript more readable. Thank you to Vikki Mackay for her support and review of the original manuscript and many friends who have given me their objective opinions and constructive criticisms.

I extend my most sincere gratitude to all the individuals who participated in my research. Many interviewees have spent countless hours sharing their life and love story with me, to help me to unravel the mystery of life and love.

Last, but not least, I am thankful to all the soulmates with whom I have a strong emotional connection in this lifetime. The heart of this book is the imprint of the life and love wisdom I've learned from you. My life would not have been complete without you. Walking this path with you has taught me what love is, and continues to make me a better person.

Introduction

N OT SURPRISINGLY, GIVEN that romance and love are important interests in my life, my favourite movies are romantic comedies and dramas. And since I'm also interested in spirituality, I loved the 1990 movie *Ghost*, in which a grieving girlfriend has an ongoing romantic relationship with her boyfriend's spirit after his death.

This movie is of course a Hollywood fairy-tale romance. Everyone knows that neither fairy tales nor Hollywood romances are grounded in truth, right? Well, I'm a person who believes the opposite. I believe that the depictions of romance we see in popular movies reflect our ideals about love, and that with intention and self-awareness it's possible to actualize those ideals in our real lives.

The way each of us perceives love, especially romantic love, is shaped by our personal worldview. Under the modern Western worldview, which is ruled by logic and scientific evidence, many moviegoers and film critics would view the premise of *Ghost* as pure fantasy, rejecting the idea that true love between two individuals can live on beyond the death of the body. But as a person whose worldview includes the concept of reincarnation, I have seen evidence that romance beyond the bounds of a human lifespan is indeed possible.

Many years ago, a man I knew died. Everyone who knew him was mourning the loss, but his stepdaughter was particularly affected by it. About a week after his death, the man's spirit returned to the earthly realm because his beloved stepdaughter's consciousness had been taken over by a hostile presence, and he wished to free her from it. I was in the room the night he stepped into her body to drive out the intruding spirit. After his stepdaughter's consciousness was restored, his spirit remained in her body long enough to tell his wife he still loved her. This man was my stepfather; his stepdaughter was my sister; and his wife was my mother.

If you greet this story with skepticism, I can understand why. I would probably have been skeptical about it, too, except that nine other people were in the room that night, and they all witnessed the same heartfelt romantic moment. That leaves me with no doubt that what I saw actually happened. With family members present, my mother and stepfather discussed personal matters that were only known between them. The specific things they said to each other have since faded from my memory, but what has remained crystal clear in my mind is the authenticity of the exchange between them.

Like most people, I have always longed for certainty that love can last, and that love can bring out the best in me, including the altruistic impulse to make sacrifices for the sake of my beloved. Many of us struggle to make this ideal a reality in our lives, and so we turn to Hollywood for solace and inspiration. But I had the honour of witnessing this type of love between my mother and stepfather, through the intermediary of my sister. It proved to me that enduring love is real.

This experience, which occurred when I was 25 years old, affected me in two ways. First, I could no longer deny that we continue to exist after our physical death. Second, I realized that love between two people exists beyond the earthly realm. The body will inevitably die, but love can live on. This realization triggered what has become a lifelong interest in seeking to understand the true nature of romantic love, the concept of an afterlife, the soul and many other mysteries.

Because I've experienced a great deal of emotional pain in relationships, as most of us have, I'm also interested in why we choose to suffer with particular people in our lives. Talking to other people about how they connect romantically only increased my curiosity. What is the meaning of the pain that love can bring? Is there an invisible force that brings two individuals together and, if so, where does it come from? Can we choose to opt out of it? *Should* we? And why are we endowed with the capacity to fall in love in the first place?

Searching for answers, I turned to Eastern, Christian and pagan traditions. Each religious tradition defines the concepts of souls and soulmates differently, and their definitions are intimately bound up with their respective worldviews and other concepts in each system. Even within our Western cultural framework, the word "soulmate" means different things to different people. Individuals who don't believe in the afterlife might define a soulmate as someone who can understand them deeply and whose traits complement their own. Or they might think of a soulmate as someone very similar to them—a close friend with whom they experience a sense of warmth and belonging they've never found with anyone else.

After all my investigation into the concepts of souls and soulmates in different spiritual traditions, I can find no single convincing hypothesis to explain different people's experiences or make sense of the romantic liaison between the spirit of my stepfather and my mother. Because every tradition sees truth, but only a partial truth, I can only synthesize my personal experiences with my research findings and the concepts I have gleaned from different spiritual traditions to develop my own philosophical framework—the existential spiritual framework I described in my first book, *Changing Fate Through Reincarnation*. Within this framework, an organic and comprehensive definition of the soulmate and true romantic love emerged.

After three decades of study and research, the clearest and most empowering definition I have found is this: A romantic soulmate is a beloved kindred spirit who inspires us across many lifetimes to continually grow into a better human being. I describe this special relationship in depth in Chapter 1.

I BEGAN MY esoteric studies in 1987 with a master of physiognomy and palmistry in Hong Kong. Upon returning to Canada in 1989, I continued my training in a range of occult traditions, including tea-leaf reading, astrology and the tarot. Between 1994 and 2004, I took courses in Eastern and Western philosophy, history, religion, psychology, sociology and anthropology at the University of British Columbia. I also began my study of Buddhism, which continues to this day.

One of the most personally impactful systems I studied is a Chinese system of divination known as the Eight Characters, which are the symbols for the year, month, day and hour of the study subject's birth. Unlike astrology, Eight Characters does not use the celestial realm as a reference point to understand a person's true nature. Instead, it uses the Chinese concept of *chi*, which means life force or energy, mapped against the geographic and temporal co-ordinates of their birth. The resulting energy chart is a blueprint of a person's past life karmic potentiality, and also provides a possible road map for their current life.

By 1995, I had embarked upon my own self-directed research program, which involved interviewing many different people from all age ranges and walks of life about their spiritual beliefs and relationships. These were not rote interviews, but deep discussions based on my interest in people, in what they believe, and in who and how they love. Using Eight Characters as my chief research tool, I constructed energy charts for the people I interviewed. By identifying discrepancies between the stories told by the interview subjects and their charts, I could identify the hidden forces in their lives, including conflicts carried over from past lives.

My energy training, which began with my study of martial arts as a teen, has continued through the practices of qigong, tai chi, yoga, and Taoist and Buddhist meditation, as well as Taoist sexual qigong and exposure to tantric sex, which helped me to understand the nature of sexual energy. Through this energy work, combined in later years with psychic training, I have opened my chakras and meridian channels to the point where I can tune into the energetic states of other people. (I will talk more about this kind of empathy later in this book.)

The philosophy of romantic love I describe in this book has grown out of these studies and practices, as well as the lessons learned from my own personal experiences. Over the years, I have crossed paths with several soulmates, and these encounters have shaped the definition of true romantic love that I am about to share. If I were to describe each of those encounters and what I learned from them in detail, this book would quickly become a memoir of my personal romantic journey rather a book that can help you understand the sacred path of the soulmate. But for the purposes of this book, the key point is that each encounter has made me reflect more deeply on why I crossed paths in this life with my soulmates, why I've experienced so much pain with them, and how the pain and joy of romantic relationships has helped me to evolve spiritually.

I do not believe we are fated to be unhappy. In the reincarnation-based worldview, it is not God that determines the course of a person's life, but the law of karma. The unexpected, often life-altering events that we might be tempted to ascribe to fate are actually the effect of actions we have taken in this life and in previous ones. According to the law of karma, if we change our conscious actions, we can change our destiny. The second important point that disproves the theory of fate is that each of us has control over our inner experience. Consciously or unconsciously, we choose how we will respond to life's events. This means that we are the creators of happiness and love, and also the creators of our own worst pain. Finally, one of the most important forces that shapes the course of our lives is our own unique blend of human qualities. Because our thoughts, assumptions, habits and personality traits guide the choices we make and actions we take, we unconsciously chart a life path that may not be in alignment with the blueprint of potentialities that we were born with. Every encounter we have has its own reasons and lessons. But the lesson my encounters as a whole have taught me is the central thesis in this book: that the relational path is a spiritual path. And I hope it will help you to understand the same thing.

The foundation of spirituality is self-awareness. We have control over many factors in life that shape our destiny, and self-awareness is one of them. The more knowledge we have about ourselves, the more options we have available to us as we choose each step on our life path. When we cultivate self-awareness to improve the quality of our life and relationships, we are practising spirituality.

Religious and spiritual material is subjective; it's always a question of investigating the ideas of great thinkers, and then comparing those ideas to what feels true in your heart. I believe the ideas in this book to be the truth of our existence. If you consider yourself a spiritual seeker, you must decide for yourself which aspects of these ideas feel resonant for you. It isn't essential to agree with all of the spiritual beliefs and theories presented in this book to find value in the messages presented here. Using these ideas as a jumping-off point into your own inner exploration can help you increase your self-awareness and gain an understanding and appreciation for the special transformative qualities that true romantic love offers.

I am not a relationship authority, nor am I a spiritual teacher. I am an existential philosopher who believes the ultimate authority in your life is yourself. I will not ask you to believe that what I say in this text is true; if something doesn't ring true to you, you're welcome to discard it. What's important to me is that you rely on your own objectivity, rationality and intuition to guide you in your own romantic and spiritual quest.

You don't even have to be interested in spirituality to get something out of this book; you may only want to find happiness in your relationships. Although my beliefs about love are rooted in my spirituality—for example, my belief in reincarnation explains a lot of things in life that otherwise have no explanation—you may be content without such an explanation. But you can still learn a lot about relationships and romantic love by seeing the relational path as a path to personal moral growth and relationship happiness within the context of a single lifetime. The important point, I believe, is that you are not fated to be unhappy or alone; you can take action to change who you are and to change the course of your life and relationships. To grow and change consciously, we must be aware that every choice we make brings with it consequences, and take responsibility for the destiny we choose.

In discussing love, romance, relationships and sex, with people of different backgrounds and beliefs, I am invariably asked how to define these concepts, and how to build a happy relationship. I respond by directing the questions back to the inquirer:

what do these concepts mean to you personally? To change within, you must be your own authority. Even though we may be inclined to conform to the prevailing definition, or according to definitions from sources we deem to be greater authorities than ourselves, we are the creators of our own relationships, and the love, sex, happiness and suffering that go along with them.

To get the most out of this book, I advise you to become aware of your own beliefs and attitudes towards love, relationships and spirituality. Only in this way will you be able to create your own romantic reality. To cultivate self-awareness as you read, I'd like to suggest three methods for self-reflection. First, monitor your own emotional responses while reading. These emotions, whether you strongly agree or disagree with the text, are messages sent to you from your higher self.

The second reflection method is to answer the questions I've included at the end of each chapter. Examining these answers, on your own or with a discussion group (which I highly recommend) will help you understand your own beliefs and attitudes towards love, relationships and spirituality.

The third reflection method is to ask your own questions. You cannot grow romantically and spiritually unless you start asking questions that are intrinsic to you and your life. And by looking at why you are asking those questions, you get to know yourself more deeply. Examine how you ascribe certain values, experiences and beliefs to the answers; how you limit your experiences by telling yourself that this is what love, sex or dating should be or must be. See whether your attitude limits your way of being and experiencing your life. Then reflect on which past experiences have shaped your attitude and the meaning you give to the answers.

ALTHOUGH THIS BOOK focuses largely on romantic relationships, my purpose in writing it is broader than that. While researching the concepts of fate, romantic love and suffering, I realized that the heartache that arises from romantic love is not only an individual challenge, but also a social issue. I believe development in our personal relationships is an important key to transforming the way each of us relates to our communities, our countries, and even our world. Anyone's concept of self, regardless of their spiritual beliefs, is the product of interdependence between them and the society around them, so effecting change within is tied to effecting change on a wider basis. All changes must be preceded by new awareness. In the epilogue of this book, I explore the idea of initiating a social movement to teach love and self-awareness skills to young people.

To facilitate change in the hearts of individuals and throughout society, I wrote *The Sacred Path of the Soulmate* as a road map to help all lovers and spiritual seekers navigate through challenging romantic terrain, and to help you, the reader, find your way home to love.

ONE

What Is a Soulmate?

Anna sinks back in her seat on the train from Vienna to Munich, caressing a wooden music box in her lap. As the train gathers speed, her thoughts move from her husband and two children, who will share a late supper with her upon her arrival, to the past three days in hotel room 408. When she lifts the lid of the music box, the tinkling sound of Moonlight Sonata fills the carriage, transporting her back to an evening five years earlier. She had been browsing in her favourite used bookstore in Vienna, Moonlight Sonata softly playing in the background, when she first locked eyes with the man who would become her secret lover. A powerful, perhaps even divine, force overcame her when she looked into his eyes. In an instant, her entire being tingled. This mystical encounter turned her life upside down.

In the 15 years Anna has been with her husband, she's never doubted that she wanted to stay with him forever. They are both *intellectuals who share common interests and are devoted to their children. They are also sexually compatible partners who know how to please each other in bed. By contrast, Anna rarely reaches orgasm with her lover, yet feels an intimacy and unity with him that she never experiences with her husband. With her lover, there is no witty repartee, but there are intimate conversations that last long into the night. He comes from a totally unfamiliar cultural background and is nearly 20 years her junior, but he makes her feel alive to her core.*

Has she gone crazy? What makes a mature, educated and happily married woman risk everything for occasional trysts in a Vienna hotel with a man half her age who is in no way a likely match for her? None of it makes sense. All Anna knows is that she cannot imagine relinquishing either relationship.

What is love? Anna wonders. Why has she fallen for her lover even though her husband meets her needs perfectly well? What is a soulmate? Is it possible to have two soulmates in one life? And if her lover really is "the one" for her, why did she not meet him before her husband? Anna searches for an explanation to ease her guilt and restore her clarity, but none comes. Now that she has known and loved these two men, she wonders how she will ever be a complete person without both of them by her side.

ANNA'S SITUATION IS a classic struggle between mind and heart, between practical considerations and romantic yearning. She cannot explain where the irresistible connection with her secret lover comes from. She only knows she has intense feelings for both men, a confusing situation that has caused her to study her own heart in a new way. Before she met her lover, she never questioned whether the affection she felt for her husband was really love, or whether love and relationship were two different things. She never wondered why love can cause great suffering as well as joy, much less whether that suffering might have a purpose. Now embroiled in an affair that defies her values and core beliefs, Anna is re-examining all this and more.

If you were a friend of Anna's, what would you counsel her to do? Would you insist she break off her affair immediately and seek counselling with her husband for the sake of their family? Or would you urge her to follow her heart and relish every moment with the young lover who makes her feel so alive?

Your answer isn't right or wrong. But it provides a key to understanding your personal beliefs about the nature of love, relationships and marriage.

A Brief History of Love and Marriage

The concept of romantic love is constantly evolving. In the West today, we believe every marriage should be built on a solid foundation of romantic love, and we feel it is our birthright to choose whom we marry. But historically, it wasn't always that way.

It's unclear how far back in history the idea of romantic love goes. But the idea of finding fulfillment through a partner goes back at least as far as ancient Greece. In his *Symposium* (385–370 BC), Plato presented the idea that humans were descended from mythical beings with three different permutations of pairs of gender (masculine and masculine, feminine and feminine, masculine and feminine), which were split in half by the gods.[1] After this, individuals were destined to find their other half on this earth, a concept that lives on in popular ideas such as that opposites attract, or when people refer to their partners as "my other half" or "my better half."

Throughout much of human history, marriage was not so much about love or romance as it was about consolidating a family's wealth and power, or carrying on its bloodlines. According to sociologist Anthony Giddens, the idea of romantic love emerged after the eighteenth century and began to incorporate notions of intimacy and sexuality. By the end of the Victorian era and the turn of the twentieth century, romantic love was increasingly associated with the freedom to follow your heart.

After World War II, the growth of globalization and capitalism began to affect every aspect of life, including romance. Many groups, including women, began to explore their rights and freedoms. The introduction of easily accessible contraception meant women were no longer held hostage by their role in reproduction, and were freer to explore their sexuality. Reproductive choice also gave women more career choice, which improved their economic standing and led to greater freedom of choice in marriage.

In the 1960s, the human potential movement, spearheaded by such humanist psychologists as Carl Rogers and Abraham Maslow, boosted the pace of transformation of Western concepts of romantic love. Men and women from all walks of life and cultural backgrounds began seeking to actualize their potential as unique individuals through therapy, encounter groups, creative pursuits and supportive partnerships.

The freedom to choose whom we love is not only historically recent, as we've seen, but culturally rare, because it's only possible in societies in which women's rights and financial independence are protected by law and social norms. Only then do women and men have the freedom to choose a particular partner, or to express themselves authentically in the relationship. In many countries, arranged marriages remain the norm, and mates are selected for the benefits they'll bring to each other's families. In societies with more traditional values and economic models, ones that emphasize the collective good over personal self-sufficiency and self-determination, individual desire may be seen as unimportant, and even as a potential threat to social order.

This is a far cry from the contemporary view that values personal happiness above all else. Choice of partner, now seen as a right in the Western world, is still beyond the reach of many individuals in developing countries where economic and gender oppression remain the norm. At the same time, in the West, expanding notions of equality are moving many to see romantic relationships as opportunities for self-actualization and healing. With this modern attitude, most of us expect a lot more from our significant other, regardless of gender. This is where the "Sacred Path" for which this book is named comes in.

Because of these high expectations, we are choosy. We won't settle down with just anyone; we want someone who has been divinely chosen as "the one." We expect this person to be a trustworthy best friend, an exciting lover, a sensitive confidante, a constant admirer, and an excellent housemate who will enthusiastically share child-rearing and domestic chores. Oh, and if they happen to give great back rubs, so much the better.

This is how many Westerners define the concept of a soulmate. If we are good people with healthy self-esteem, the theory goes, God or the Universe will reward us with our soulmate, and we will live happily ever after.

Redefining the Soulmate

Definitions of the soul vary, but I am defining it for our purposes as the spiritual part of a human being, usually regarded as immortal. The concept of the soulmate, and related concepts such as reincarnation and karma, have been studied for centuries in many cultures, including Western ones. Reincarnation was included in early Christian doctrine, although it was discarded at the first Council of Nicaea in 325 AD.[2] In spite of that, a few Christian sects, such as Christian Cabbalists and Rosicrucians, still believe in it.[3] And surveys show that a large percentage of self-identified Christians in the United States believe in reincarnation.[4]

More recently, the concept of reincarnation took on new life, so to speak, with the publication of Michael Newton's 1994 bestseller *Journey of Souls*.[5] According to Newton's theory, each soul belongs to a primary group of souls made up of about 15 spirits.

Each soul also affiliates with a number of secondary soul groups, which are organized hierarchically in the spirit realm based on their level of moral maturity.

Newton also believes souls tend to travel in groups when they return to Earth from the spiritual realm. Because they shared experiences in their previous lives in the material world, and have close connections in their primary and secondary soul groups, upon meeting each other in new incarnations these souls feel immediately familiar. Sexless in the spirit world, they are nonetheless able to choose to incarnate in male or female form. They are also able to choose the family they will be born into, basing their choice of parents upon past-life connections. (Some New Age followers believe that soulmates in each group switch social roles from one Earth life to the next, and could therefore be incarnated as a parent, grandparent, friend, lover, sibling or nemesis.) Whatever the past or current arrangement, we meet in human form again and again to learn the moral lessons necessary for our spiritual growth, which is what gives life purpose.

Past-Life Experiences and Memories

To understand how our impressions and memories carry forward from one life to the next, let's turn to Eastern theory—in particular, to the Mere Consciousness school in Mahayana Buddhism.

A sect of Mahayana Buddhism, the Mere Consciousness school originated in India during the fourth century AD.[6] It teaches that there are eight aspects of consciousness: the five senses and three more. The sixth is our conceptual mind (or perception); the seventh, self-awareness, is awareness of ourselves as separate entities, and the eighth is storehouse consciousness, a memory bank that stores all emotional thoughts and ideas we've collected across our lifetimes. The seventh and eighth aspects of consciousness jointly house the divine essence of the soul. In Mahayana Buddhism, this divine essence is called one's Buddha nature.

At our highest and purest level, we are all one, a unified field of creative consciousness that has no opposite and no enemy. While our souls are specific and particular, our divine nature is whole, perfect and universal. Clearly, humans are far from perfect in our thoughts and actions. We all behave in ways that are hurtful and harmful to ourselves and others from time to time, and some people are worse than others in this way. Sadly, humanity is filled with episodes of unkindness and even cruelty. These impulses stem from the fact that we feel separate from one another, and this sense of separation breeds fear, judgment, defensiveness and the impulse to attack. We do not know that our true nature is one of love and unity. Our divine qualities are always present, but it is as though they are obscured or distorted by impurities in our personality structure, in the same way a cloudy sky obscures the sun.

Our purpose in returning to Earth to live as a human being is to purify this personality structure through a series of developmental stages. The more advanced a person's moral development, the more easily divine qualities such as love, compassion and a sense of interconnectedness flow through them.

Because each soul's structure is unique in its blend of attributes, its response to life is different and requires different stimuli from one person to the next, and from each Earth life to the next. This means the core aspects of our soul, the foundation of our being, manifests in a unique way, which characterizes our individuality. In a nutshell, although we are born into a new body in every life, shaped by the experiences and conditions in which we live, the underlying structure of each unique soul is continuous from one incarnation to the next. This means that the past life attitudes accrued in the soul memory become potential or actual personality traits in subsequent incarnations.

For example, one person has a tendency to do things at the last minute. Another person has a strong will. The third person has an ability to foresee unpleasant events. All these individuals have had these unique tendencies and abilities since childhood. Their parents did not influence them to develop these traits. Rather, they simply came "wired" that way.

Just as these traits are carried forward from one life to the next, they are carried forward in this life from one day to the next. Sleep can be viewed as a metaphor for a daily death. So if Tommy went to bed last night with a weak sense of morality and over-sensitive heart, he wakes up with the same qualities the next morning.

As we move from one incarnation to another, our past-life learned experiences accompany us, stored in the eighth aspect of our consciousness. These seeds store the flavour of relational experiences with particular souls in past lives, and carry them forward to the current life. To manifest the full force of these stored past-life experiences, these seeds must interact with the environment. The above two potential qualities in Tommy would not manifest if the environment did not stimulate them. Thus, nurturing and the environment are important in shaping the person's development. The strength of all traits in Tommy, especially potential traits, can be weakened or modified in each life.

This theory explains the interplay of past-life conditioning and current-life experiences that make us who we are. If a person is born with low self-esteem due to their soul's personality structure, and if they choose to be born into an abusive family, their childhood conditions could trigger the development of dysfunctional habits and addiction in their current life. By the same token, by choosing life conditions that bring out our pre-existing unresolved issues, we are also inviting the opportunity to confront, challenge and eventually heal them. How we feel about certain people we encounter depends on our stored past-life experiences. Because past-life memories, including those of romantic love, can carry forward, a person may feel innate attraction (or its opposite, dislike or even repulsion) toward certain individuals or even groups of people.

So while in popular psychological theory, two forces (nature and nurture) shape the development of personality, a reincarnation worldview adds a third force—the memories of past-life experiences, values and emotions. Nature and nurture act on the seeds of personality traits carried forward from past lives to make a person who they are in each life.

The Merits of Buddhism

I am not a believer of any world religion. However, I have respect for Buddhism because it is a philosophy built on the concepts of self-responsibility and cause and effect. My theories pay homage to Buddhism because there is no room for fatalism in Buddhism. How we respond to life is determined by our own selves. In this philosophy, we always have a choice.

Although it appears that Tommy was born with weak morality and emotional over-sensitivity, this is not predisposed by genes or by God. The causes of Tommy's weaknesses are the actions he has undertaken and the choices he has made. If, today, when Tommy wakes up, he is aware he has these tendencies, he can make efforts to change how he thinks, feels and acts. If Tommy makes different choices today, his life will be different tomorrow, including its romantic aspects.

If you are a follower of a particular religion or a die-hard supporter of science, you might see your life as fated to be a certain way. However, seen through the lens of Buddhism, there is always hope in life if we see who we are and why we are. Buddhists believe there is a way out of the suffering caused by our un-awakened minds. I go into greater detail about how past-life conditioning can carry to the future lives in my earlier book *Changing Fate Through Reincarnation.*[7]

Our past life memory affects four key areas of the romantic

experience: who we are attracted to; who we fall in love with; the strength of our attachment to them; and how we cope with a broken heart. We will deal with each of these in subsequent chapters.

This also raises a possible theory about the roots of same-sex attraction and transgender identity. True romantic love has no gender biases. We have all been in many different bodies and relationship types with our soulmates. In the reincarnation worldview, some souls' sexual orientation is strongly influenced by their past-life memories. For example, imagine that you have lived many lives in female bodies. Your habit in your past lives was to have most, or all, of your sexual experiences with male partners. Although you are in a male body in your current life, you are attracted to other males due to the power of memory. Going a step further, if your attachment to gender identity from past lives is extremely strong, you may feel that the body you're in now does not reflect your true gender, in which case you might identify as transgender.

Sexuality is frequently understood to be biological and gender, sociological. In the reincarnation model, all sexual preferences are natural. What is not natural are the prejudices in our minds and the ignorance of some attitudes toward sexual orientation. Society needs to advance its thinking to accelerate the awakening of the global consciousness around this situation.

Returning to Love

Love is the substance from which we were formed and the home from which we came. The purpose of life is to undertake the journey home; to merge with the unified field of creative consciousness. To do this, we need to transform the impure energy that clogs up the Buddha nature in each of our souls. At the earlier stages of the developmental journey, we are prone to making all sorts of mistakes, sometimes with devastating consequences. But despite our many shortcomings and blind spots, we all instinctively agree on the qualities that define human goodness, such as compassion, fairness, generosity, kindness and love. That tells us something about our unchanging core nature.

We return to this earthly plane because it is in physical form that our souls are best able to learn the spiritual lessons we need to learn and cannot learn in the spirit world. Because we are spirits incarnate as human beings, it follows that spiritual growth and humanistic growth are closely intertwined, if not one and the same. By healing our human wounds and dysfunction, we grow closer to our own divine essence. And because this is a co-evolutionary process—that is, one in which we must evolve together rather than in isolation—we need other people to help us grow. Understood from this perspective, a soulmate is simply someone we have known in past lives who helps us to grow in our evolutionary journey.

Because the work of spiritual evolution is complex and challenging, it can take lifetimes to make real progress. (The universe is in no rush.) We all have many soulmates with whom we meet up again and again from one lifetime to the next. Each time we meet, we pick up where we left off. This explains the instant feelings of kinship we sometimes feel when we first meet people who later become our close friends, and also explains what is often referred to as "love at first sight," which we will explore in depth in Chapter 3.

Romantic Soulmates

One role that has a great deal of power to shape our human qualities is the soulmate with whom we share feelings of love, sexual passion and attachment. Taken together, these three qualities are the essential ingredients of what most people would define as romantic love. Our romantic soulmate is a special kind of soulmate because with them we have a deep, yet non-familial, connection that involves sex, powerful yearning and voluntary attachment. Falling in love creates a special energetic state in which our higher selves come alive. The type of lessons we learn in romantic relationships with a soulmate are different, and potentially more profound, than the lessons we need to learn from other soulmates who play different social roles in our lives.

Sometimes we work with multiple romantic soulmates in a single lifetime. When more than one soulmate appears as a potential romantic partner at the same time, the conflict can pull us in different directions, as in Anna's dilemma at the top of this chapter. But this painful, chaotic moment offers a kernel of deep spiritual wisdom from which we can learn.

Viewed through this lens, it's clear that the forces at work in Anna's dilemma are even more complex than they appear on the surface. It's true that she loves her husband and is devoted to her family. But her secret lover brings qualities to her life that open her up in ways she needs in order to grow.

Anna has had a fine companionship with her husband. They are good cohabitants who share a dry, sarcastic sense of humour, enjoy cooking together and are highly compatible in bed. But as Anna matures, she is developing a yearning for things she is not getting in her relationship with her husband. Anna was not even aware of this longing in herself until she met her lover, a man so gentle and non-judgmental that he caused her to question her own nature, to ask herself things like what it means to be a kind person, what it feels like to let down her guard and allow herself to be vulnerable and open. Simply by being himself, Anna's lover is making her want to grow. If she were to turn away from him, she would be turning away from a beautiful emerging aspect of herself. But if she were to turn away from her husband, she would be turning away from the life they have created and the dreams that they had been building toward together.

A Sacred Path

Although several kinds of soulmate relationships can help with our spiritual growth, I believe that romantic soulmate relationships are our primary vehicle for this growth. There are three reasons for this.

First, romantic soulmate relationships are driven not only by love but also a powerful urge to merge with another being. This encourages the journey of the soul from isolation, fear and egoistic thinking toward oneness and divine qualities. Interpersonal relationships provide the best possible environment and stimulus to grow through our issues and heal psychological wounds because all relationship dysfunction is an error that exists on the level of the personality; it is not part of our essential true nature. Simply put, relationships are the curriculum through which we learn to love.

Second, romantic love is universal. Many other practices, such as meditation, prayer, asceticism, prostration, religious study and contemplation promise to cultivate spiritual development. But romantic love is a more potent, powerful and important path than any of these precisely because it transcends religion, belief systems and ideology.

Conveniently, it also happens to be linked to the continuation of the species. Relationships are sought by virtually every person on Earth, regardless of their culture, religion or belief system. In this way, romantic love can be seen as the universe's mechanism to ensure that every human being has an opportunity (and innate urge) to grow and evolve as a spiritual being—even those who don't believe in God or the existence of the soul.

Third, romantic love is a journey of awakening, in which we move from unconsciousness to consciousness, from the errors of the ego-mind to the self-awareness of the soul. We will go into how this works in much greater depth in Chapter 3.

Viewed another way, the concept of "soulmate" can be taken to mean that we mate with our own soul in a reintegration of self. Our souls come back to this dimension to join with other soulmates to learn spiritual lessons that we have not learned well yet, but the journey toward unity really begins within. Through the external connection with our soulmate, we gradually become self-aware. Our body, mind and soul become one, a necessary step before we can have harmonic unity on the spiritual plane.

Every sacred path leads to the same destination, regardless of its origin or the route taken. Spiritual seekers and love seekers alike will arrive home to love when they experience unity and compassion for themselves and others. This occurs both in the socio-psychological realm and energetically in the spiritual realm.

The purpose of life is to return to the love from which we came. In simple terms, we are on a life journey to discover our authentic self, which embodies our soul essence. If we let it, true romantic love can change our hearts and our minds in ways that leave the world a better place simply because we were here.

FURTHER CONSIDERATION

- If you were a friend of Anna's, would you advise her to let go of her lover and stay with her husband, let go of her husband and stay with her lover, continue the affair in secrecy, or relocate to the far north and live in an ice hut so she won't have to think about such difficult things? (Just kidding.) What would your reasons be for the advice you'd give to Anna?

- In the text, a soulmate is defined as a soul with whom you've had close, though not necessarily romantic, contact in a past life. Does this definition fit for you? If not, how would you define "soulmate"?

- If you are currently in a romantic relationship, do you feel it has made/is making you into a better person? In what ways? Do you feel it's making your partner into a better person? In what ways? If you're not currently in a relationship, consider this question with regard to a past relationship.

- What lessons do you think you might be here to learn in this life? What life experiences have you had that make you think so? Assuming you're right, how would you evaluate your progress so far? What might you need to do to make more progress?

- How do you feel about same-sex relationships and transgender identity? Might the thoughts in this chapter cause you to think about them differently?

- Do you believe life, in general, has a purpose? If so, what is it? Have the ideas in this chapter inspired any new thoughts about that? Do you believe *your life* specifically has a purpose? What do you think it is?

- Do you have any idiosyncratic traits that have been present since childhood? If yes, where do you think these unique traits come from?

TWO

The Spiritual Purpose of True Romantic Love

As the airplane touches down at the New Delhi International airport, you feel your heart pound with anxiety. Lately, there has been a lot of news about women travellers being assaulted in India, and this is your first big solo journey. Ahead looms a three-hundred-kilometre bus trip to the ashram and you don't know what to expect—from this journey or from your future. "What am I doing?" you think. "I'm a thirty-something white woman from America in this foreign land going on a meditative retreat to find my spiritual self. I had everything in life: a good-looking husband, an upscale two-bedroom apartment in Manhattan, a stellar career and a supportive community with a lot of good friends. I lacked nothing." Yet you find a huge hole in your heart and feel lost and confused.

On Christmas morning you told your husband that you wanted a divorce. A few days later, you quit your job. Now, six weeks later, not knowing where you found the courage, you have landed in this foreign country to seek your spirituality, and you are filled with hope of finding inner peace, a balanced self and true love.

IF YOU IDENTIFY with the person described above, have you ever wondered why you would need to go to an exotic place to find your spiritual self? If it's possible to find your spiritual self in a faraway land, why not in your own country? If you can only find your spirituality by spending a lot of money, what kind of spirituality are you seeking? Being spiritual doesn't mean abandoning your common sense. You can find your balanced self through spiritual practice right here at home and without emptying your bank account.

But what does that have to do with romantic love? Many people turn to spirituality for answers after enduring a painful breakup or because their love life feels empty. When they can't or don't experience a sense of love and oneness in their relationships, they turn to spiritual awakening seeking essentially the same feeling. Many mystical traditions require practitioners to retreat to a monastery and renounce worldly desires in their quest for enlightenment, as if transcendence can only be experienced in the altered state that mystics spend years learning to master. But if this were true, living day to day would have no inherent meaning.

Unless you're ready to renounce all worldly desires, including heartfelt romantic love, the question you need to ask is: "How can my idea of spirituality help me find a special connection that will create a blissful lifetime relationship?" Eastern practices certainly have their place, but can holding a yoga posture, doing qigong or tai chi, or practising breath work in an Indian ashram transform your romantic fate? Or is there a spiritual purpose in romantic love itself? The answer is definitely yes, because the relational path is a spiritual path in which we develop and refine our humanistic qualities.

The idea that we have to quit work, fly halfway around the world and spend a small fortune to find inner peace evolved over the last half-century in affluent Western countries. Eastern thought, especially Buddhist and Taoist approaches, made its way to the West in the 1960s. It brought new perspectives on the role consciousness plays in spiritual practice and emphasized the use of meditation to cultivate an altered state.

In the 1980s, a new spiritual industry sprang to life. Many spiritual teachers combined Eastern-based spirituality, with its rich knowledge of cultivating stillness, with psychological and relationship counselling on how to be less judgmental, more forgiving and accepting, or how to deal with addiction issues, and so on. Paid courses on meditation, yoga and exercises to release emotional and sexual blockages began popping up. Expensive online personal-development workshops and retreats in luxury resorts became the modern trend in spiritual enlightenment.

But paying a hefty price to hear a popular spiritual teacher speak is not necessary to improving your conceptual and experiential understanding of spirituality. If you want the equivalent of spiritual fast food, psychedelic drugs such as those used in an ayahuasca ceremony may satisfy your immediate needs.[1] But this contemporary way of paying a fee to experience an ancient ritual—dropping in and taking a herb, or inhaling incense and chanting, while remaining outside of the culture in which these ancient spiritual practices are embedded—has little to do with connecting to the divine.

More importantly, this pay-to-play attitude sidesteps the reason for connecting with divine love, which is simply to experientially understand that the purpose of life is to return to the love from which we came. We don't need to participate in expensive or exotic rituals to learn this. Can a hallucinatory journey help a spiritual seeker to turn the other cheek when hurt? Is a journey to an ashram more likely to make the seeker understand the role of fidelity in their relationships than simple daily contemplation? Can sitting in a lotus position transform a negative self-image into healthy self-esteem that helps the seeker cultivate fulfillment in their career and love life?

Every relationship reflects the human qualities of the two partners who create it. The kind of human qualities we bring into a relationship reflect our level of maturity. If energetic practices and psychedelic drugs could transmute two lovers' human qualities, there would be no need for therapy, life coaching or family counselling. There would be no need to confront our pain and do recovery work.

Energetic practices are vital and indispensable in our spiritual journey, as these trainings have positive psychological and energetic effects. Psychedelic drugs and ayahuasca drinking can bring seekers instant divine experiences, which can have profound impacts on their self-concept and the true nature of the universe. Yet it's not enough; it's also essential to do some soul searching, to ask yourself about the extent to which the practices in your spiritual quest will change the human qualities which are the source of both your pains and your happiness. A spiritual journey is a developmental journey in which we have to do the work to transform the negative human qualities into wholesome and virtuous human qualities.

Are you looking for love? If so, you need to know what that means to you. There is no art but what is within the artist. Likewise, there is no love but what is within the person. Our human qualities create the connections that serve as the conduits for love. Love, which is another word for divinity, exists within each of us. We need only lift the veil to reveal its beauty.

If love is embodied in our human qualities, we need to cultivate our human qualities. The training ground in spirituality is in relationship with ourselves, others and life to transform our negative aspects and our dysfunctional, conditional selves into something better, something more loving and divine. But this cannot happen in a vacuum. We need the environment and the people around us, especially our romantic partners, to help us grow. In the last fifty years, human consciousness has evolved so dramatically that romantic love has become a key spiritual tool—if not *the* key spiritual tool—enabling us to evolve. But before I explain the nuts and bolts of the spiritual component in contemporary romantic love, I need to provide you with a better theoretical understanding of why human life itself is the training ground for spirituality.

A Glimpse of the Divine

According to Buddhist tradition, enlightenment requires one to transform their human qualities to the point where they have a pure heart/mind and thus pure desires, which is an extremely difficult journey. Human qualities can only be transformed by actions and choices that embody our desires and values.

This is where the concept of love fits into spiritual development. Twenty-five-hundred years ago, Buddha taught an ascetic path designed to purify the heart, mind and spirit. For Buddha, this meant divorcing himself from his family and pursuing a monastic lifestyle. But the relational path—which I consider a hidden, or less obvious, path because it is buried within the concept of love—leads to the same end. Although the meanings of romance and love change over time to reflect contemporary values and social challenges, the unconditional love and goodness that are fundamental to our true nature do not. For example, in the Christian tradition, God is love, which is the basis of being and the source of all love. No matter what our religious or spiritual beliefs, when we embed love in all our actions and choices, we purify our hearts, minds and spirits.

We don't need to spend large sums of money or take mind-altering substances to learn this; the only surefire way to learn about spirituality is to enroll in the hands-on university called life, which is free. Life is a web of relationships in which love resides, and one of the most important relationships we will ever create in life is a romantic love relationship. For many of us, relationships are conditional because we want our lovers to meet our needs and desires. When two people bring different needs, desires, values and pasts into a relationship, tension and conflict can arise. But that's all right, because the spiritual purpose in a romantic love relationship is to use the struggle of a conditional relationship as a vehicle through which to transmute our human qualities and become better people.

In a true romantic love relationship, we forge a new identity with our romantic partner to create a life that reflects who we want to be. In the course of cultivating the love relationship through an increasingly integrated body, mind, heart and spirit, we:

1. Attune and connect with ourselves.
2. Attune and connect with our partners.
3. Attune and connect with life.

When these three levels of attunement and connection are aligned, we live consciously in a state of existential unity, which embodies cosmic unity. The vehicle for cosmic unity is love. Like spirituality, love itself is a state of pure consciousness—a power that can drive transformation. Love in its broadest sense is the mother of romantic love, which is a special state in which two lovers experience social, psychological, erotic, materialistic and mystical fusion. Romantic love can enable two lovers to use their relationship to transform their human qualities and thus fuse two consciousnesses into one. How we experience love is the reflection of how conscious we are as we live our lives.

True romantic love originates from our soul. The love we are searching for is our own divine quality. It is our spiritual nature to seek connections over and above those that meet our reproductive, social, economic and psychological needs. Love is a power that binds humanity together. Romantic love connects two individuals, whereas universal love connects everyone. True romantic love can work like magic to instantly transform us. We can transform in small ways, or we can experience quantum leaps in our spiritual growth.

In my experience, true romantic love has the following characteristics:

1. True romantic love can give us the power to grow and change into better, humbler people who experience love more purely than ever before.

2. True romantic love has the power to heal, is the source of compassion, courage, faith and confidence, and is unconditional.

3. As everyone participates in romantic relationships, true romantic love is a spiritual practice that spans all philosophies and levels of spiritual awareness or development.

Becoming Better and Humbler

In the 1956 classic *The Art of Loving*, Erich Fromm notes that the quality of true love is reflected by the human qualities that produced it; he extols the ultimate expression of love in the form of Christian universal love.[2] I would take that a step further and say that true romantic love helps us to become better, humbler people by transforming the egocentric "I" to the universal "We."

With a deeper awareness of the intimate relationship between spirituality, life and romantic love, we can transform our fate by using insightful, competent, compassionate therapists, life coaches, healers, friends or open-minded religious persons to help us tailor our spiritual, social, psychological, physical and energetic practices to our own unique needs. We can design a developmental program to grow and change. In the midst of this restoring and rebalancing process, we open our hearts with courage to let the universe take us where our souls need to travel. That state of openness is the contact point of true romantic love, which happens by chance. All the healing work is to prepare for an experience of oneness with another person that we can only stumble into.

Falling in true romantic love can be a spiritual awakening in which a new sense of self emerges instantly. There is a moment of recognition in true romantic love when we can see something deeper about life or ourselves that evokes in us a desire to change. Love creates a new self when a person suddenly feels a profound internal shift in their consciousness, a compelling urge to be good and do good.

An example of how love can spur spiritual growth can be found in one of the romantic comedies I enjoy so much, the 1997 movie *As Good As It Gets*. In the film, Jack Nicholson plays Melvin Udall, a man with severe obsessive-compulsive disorder (OCD) as well as a negative attitude that alienates others. The only person who can put up with him is waitress Carol Connelly, played by Helen Hunt. A single mom raising a son with chronic, life-threatening asthma, Carol becomes romantically involved with Melvin after he helps her out financially with one of her son's health crises. Early in their relationship, he offers her an uncharacteristically genuine statement: *You make me want to be a better man.* Carol remarks on it as the best compliment of her life, and the line goes down in Hollywood history.

True romantic love is a power that makes Melvin want to be a better person. So what does it mean to be a better person? For one thing, it means our personality will be transformed. Here I jump from Eastern to Western wisdom, for truth that transcends culture. The Bible says, "Love is patient; love is kind; love is not envious or boastful or arrogant or rude. It does not insist on its own way; it is not irritable or resentful; it does not rejoice in wrongdoing, but rejoices in the truth. It bears all things, believes all things, hopes all things, endures all things. Love never ends."[3]

Abandoning Arrogance

In Christianity, the mother of all sins is pride because it sets us furthest from God. (It's important to note that pride, when it refers to self-respect, can be positive. But what we are speaking about here is the "deadly sin" of pride, which has a negative connotation indicating arrogance and elevating ourselves above others, even God.) People with too much pride tend to disconnect from the divine qualities within themselves. Ironically, their pride gives rise to feelings of both superiority and inferiority. An air of superiority can lead to alienating others, thereby cutting us off from important social bonds, including love. The prideful person loves him- or herself, and no one else.

True romantic love, on the other hand, is about inclusion. With the blessing of true romantic love, we surrender our prideful ways. The hallmark of true romantic love is caring. To love, we must transform our pride and human weakness in the process of creating relationships with ourselves and others, to expand our sense of self to include our beloved in our lives.

Blessed with true romantic love, we surrender our protective armour, open our heart and fuse with the soul of our beloved to create a shared reality. Naturally, this inclusion leads to caring, as our beloved is part of our new identity. We care for our partner's well-being as much as we care for ourselves, if not more. If we cannot even surrender our pride to our romantic partner, and if we have no moral courage to amend our wrongs, how can we suddenly find the desire to care for others in the name of universal love, especially people whom our culture tells us are our enemies? If religious and intellectual thinkers preach universal love, but cannot see that the road to the utopia of Christian love begins at home, they are only spouting empty theories.

Opening Our Eyes

An additional blessing of true romantic love is that it opens our eyes to different kinds of love around us, and inspires us to be equally loving in all our relationships.

In Turkey, I once met a woman who demonstrated such patience, gentleness and kindness in the way she treated her older sister that it moved me deeply and the memory has never left me. Although I've seen others show the same qualities on occasion, those instances have never resonated with me in the same way. Because of this woman's patience and kindness, I felt more deeply about the biblical passage, "Love is patient, love is kind..." I felt a moral awakening inside me. If love is defined as empowering people to experience moral growth and change, it can be experienced in all life situations, independent of romantic love.

True romantic love can also help us find clarity. As humans, we are slaves to multiple and often conflicting desires and needs, which can make our hearts impure and fill us with confusion and tension. Is it ever okay to marry for security rather than love? Should a person who wants children choose to be with someone they love, even though their loved one doesn't want or can't provide children?

In true romantic love, devoting our beings to one cause or one person can consume our whole consciousness. We make fewer demands on life and our beloved. When we are in the state of being in love, what we want most is reciprocity and to be with that person even though our beloved may be poor or somehow impaired. When we are with our beloved here and now, the peace we experience makes us feel we are home. True romantic love helps us to be fully present. The purer our heart, the less we demand of our beloved in the future, and the more we focus on what we have now. With this purity, what we want most is simply to be with and nurture the one we care for the most.

True Romantic Love Is a Life Anchor

Why does life sometimes feel so empty? Why do we sometimes feel there is nothing important to live for? The magic of true romantic love is that loving a special someone ignites our passions. Because this special someone matters to us, we are willing to sacrifice a lot for this person, perhaps even our life. Sometimes we don't know how much our beloved means to us until an external circumstance tests the strength of our love—a situation that forces us to make a choice between our personal interests and the welfare of our loved one. However, if the feeling we call love for our significant other is true romantic love, it would not be a choice we'd need to make. It is a force that springs up voluntarily and naturally from the deepest corner of our soul to care for our partners. It simply happens.

For example, say you meet the love of your life and your courtship is smooth sailing. You know you want to share the rest of your life with this person. You love them more than anything. You marry and have two beautiful children. You enjoy the lifestyle you both want. On top of all this, you find that you can turn the thing you're most passionate about into a successful career. You see that by putting in time, energy and effort, you will have the money, power, status and fame you want. Because your partner is proud of you and adores you, you work harder to achieve everything so you can share the fruits of your labour with your beloved.

But, one day, you find out that your partner has a form of cancer that is very difficult to treat. Doctors cannot say how long they will live. Uncertainty hangs on your consciousness. Everything changes. Now you have a dilemma: you must choose between your worldly ambitions or devoting your time fully to your partner's medical needs. If it's true romantic love you feel, you will not weigh the pros and cons. You will not hesitate to put your emerging career on hold. You would rather spend your time with your partner in your doctor's consulting room or library researching every possible medical treatment that might cure your partner's disease. Visiting hours do not apply to you as the hospital literally becomes your second home. You cannot tell whether a day or a week or a month passes you by in hospital. The limits on your partner's life sharpen your focus on what you have together now, making you treasure it all the more.

Amid all the emotional and physical pain, you find a deeper level of intimacy. Every small thing that happens between the two of you has meaning. In the face of death and uncertainty, you feel how fortunate you are simply to hold hands together while watching the sunset on the beach. You feel you are fighting, not for your partner's survival, but for both of you. You truly feel a part of your beloved's experiences as if they are not a separate person. Your partner's pains are your pains. Your partner's depression is your depression. The true romantic love you share has dissolved the psychic boundary between you.

Love Heals

The feeling you experience around your heart region is more than a sensation. It is a power from your soul that enables you to get in touch with the humanity we all share with others at the deepest level. This power is above and beyond the pleasure principle we use to operate in our daily lives. Love has the power to transform our needs, desires and pride. Love gives us strength to endure.

All of us experience hurt, which makes us feel fragmented, as though our behaviours, thoughts, emotions, words, bodies, hearts and spirits are not in unity. We lose the sense of being anchored to the divine within us. We feel disconnected from our souls, and we disconnect from others.

In her 1987 book *Hands of Light: A Guide to Healing Through the Human Energy Field,* healer Barbara Ann Brennan wrote,

"Health not only means health in the physical body, but also balance and harmony in all parts of life. The process of healing is a process of remembering who you are. The word 'remembering' can be seen as re-membering—literally, putting the members of the body back together after hurt has torn them apart."[4] True romantic love can help us re-member ourselves—to renew trust in ourselves and in life. But this can only happen if the love we receive is pure and unconditional. Love that is patient, kind and caring brings out the seeds of the healing power within us. It gives our beloved the power to show us that true and unconditional romantic love exists in the world, and it gives us the courage to believe it.

When your lover shows you unconditional kindness, they empower you to love and respect yourself again. The trust between you empowers you to heal your brokenness and strive for wholeness again.

But true romantic love can happen only when two persons stay engaged in the process, when the unconditional love you feel from your beloved shows you that there is another way, a better way, to live and experience the world. True romantic love is the best form of therapy I know of. It can even help with relationship addiction, a topic we'll explore in depth in Chapter 7.

Poverty of the Spirit and Addiction

True and unconditional romantic love may be more important to life in the twenty-first century than at any other time in history.

Change is happening more and more quickly, not just in terms of technology and politics but also in relationships and attitudes. As cultures evolve and intermingle, we ask more questions than our forebears did and do not always have the comfort of looking to tradition for answers. Nothing seems certain, least of all our own feelings.

It is part of the human condition to create relationships. Yet with the advent of postmodern and feminist consciousness, the nature of relationships has changed. Many now see relationships as part of the means to the end of self-actualization. Who we want to be in a relationship with has become one of the most significant matters in Western modern life.

That notion has not developed as a random coincidence but as part of a collective societal shift over the last half-century. From the perspective of Joseph Campbell, the American mythologist best known for his broadcast series and book *The Power of Myth*, self-actualization is part of the hero's journey that begins with separation.[5] The hero ventures into the unknown to discover who they are, eventually returning to the community to make their contribution. This narrative is well received in the Western intellectual community because the hero's journey echoes the self-reliance, freedom and individuation that are the hallmarks of Western values and beliefs. This story arc is reflected in many influential cultural works, including George Lucas's hugely successful *Star Wars* franchise.

I believe that, since the end of World War II, Campbell's concept—that growth requires separation from and return to the community—has had an unintended hand in another social epidemic: addiction. Over the last five or six decades, an expectation that young adults should leave home to seek their identity in higher education has become the Western cultural norm. Some young minds are primed for the challenge, but many are not psychologically ready for this sudden independence. To ease the resulting anxiety and pain, many young people unconsciously develop different forms of addiction to cope.

The causes of addiction are both external and internal. Moreover, there are two categories of addiction: substance addictions and process addictions, which include love, sex and relationship addiction. Overall, addictions have been aggressively attacking our society for more than 50 years. I agree with Bruce Alexander's theory that addiction is not an individual challenge but a global social, cultural, economic and political problem. In his ground-breaking book, *The Globalization of Addiction: A Study in Poverty of the Spirit*, Alexander writes about a psychological disintegration originating from economic, social and cultural dislocation. In Alexander's words, this dislocation is called "poverty of the spirit."[6]

Poverty of the spirit is induced by rapid change and significant disparities, constraints and uncertainties in the economic, social and cultural way of life in the West. This creates tremendous stress, which in turn evokes feelings of loneliness, anxiety, emptiness and despair. For many of us, the best way to counteract this dreadful feeling is to find a deeper sense of belonging in intimate relationships. Love relationships have become a physical, psychological and spiritual sanctuary. It is not surprising, then, that many of us define our soulmates as confidantes and compassionate friends, and want unconditional love as a healing tool. That's why, I believe, a flourishing romantic love relationship may now play a more significant role in our mental and emotional health than ever before.

With the emphasis on self-reliance, freedom and individuation in the West, young people are expected to leave home to create their own identities. They find that life is an adventure full of uncertainties and surprises, and one of the most significant adventures they will ever undertake is a romantic adventure. In our culture, they rely entirely on themselves to choose a lifetime partner, to pair up with a special person to explore life and each other, to explore the spiritual and humanistic awakening experience of true romantic love. However, there is no guarantee where this romantic adventure will end. Ideally, their destination on this journey will be not only personal happiness but personal maturity, in the form of a deeper connection with themselves, their community and life.

As they go through life, young people face two distinct levels of stress: external or social stress and internal or psychological stress. These are endemic to twenty-first-century life. The social stress caused by economic and cultural dislocation affect everyone differently and can take a tremendous toll on intimate relationships. For example, a person might be preparing to settle down with their lifetime partner when the company they work for is bought out by a foreign company, which offers them a job in Asia. Do they relocate, which means giving up the relationship with their partner, who has their own career to worry about? Or do they turn down the opportunity, which could have professional and financial ramifications for years to come? Another example involves the cost of urban real estate, which may be so high that the combined income between them and their partner is not enough to afford a decent property for a family of four. The constant financial stress strains their intimate relationship. Long hours and highly stressful last-minute deadline work does not allow them to take their daughter to kung fu class or their son to dance lessons. And energy for sex and pillow talk with their partner is a thing of the past.

Faced with external pressures such as work and money, combined with feelings of alienation and loneliness, many people who lack emotional resilience develop addictive behaviours, which bankrupt their spirits and their relationships. Because many people have little understanding of addiction—especially the process addictions of love, sex and relationships—they may suffer for decades without knowing that they have an addiction issue. By the time they ask for help, they may have invested in their addictive behaviour patterns for their whole adult lives, making it that much more difficult to free themselves.

Alexander's insights into addictions connect to the central thesis of this book, spiritual awakening. I firmly believe we can use all relationships, especially romantic relationships, to develop our capacity for self-awareness. Self-awareness is the fundamental building block of resilience and maturity, guiding us to restore and rebalance our spirits amid constant pressure from economic and social dislocation.

Changing the World

Growth requires separation. Part of the maturation process is differentiating ourselves from our family of origin in order to grow into ourselves as individuals. The voluntary separation young people undertake when they embark on this adventure requires self-awareness. However, in our culture, many people set out on this adventure to choose their mates long before they've adequately matured for the task. It is hardly surprising that, when people are expected to take lifelong responsibility for the choices they make before they are ready, pain and anxiety ensue, addictions follow, and then broken relationships follow upon that. This disjointed process does not only mean our young people pay a price as they go through their lives. It means we all pay a price, and that price is both psycho-spiritual and material. Psycho-spiritually, when people struggle with unhappiness because of relationship crises, their sense of emotional brokenness ripples out to those around them. Materially, people who feel broken are less productive than those who feel whole; they care less about their work, take more sick days, and they are simply unable to contribute to their communities in optimal ways.

The point is that the pain from failed romantic adventures, terminated marital relationships and broken families is not only an individual challenge but a social issue. But the social costs we're paying for this epidemic of unhappy relationships could be forestalled if we were to begin providing relationship, self-awareness and love education—how to cultivate special human bonds with balanced mental and emotional health—to our school-aged children.

Improved self-awareness and love education could not only make future generations kinder to those around them but could help them make better choices, lead and govern more wisely, contribute more to their communities and inspire others. This type of education could have a positive impact not only on individuals and societies in the West, but across the world, creating a ripple effect that would elevate our economic, political and social consciousness globally. With the growth of global consciousness, many people in the industrial world would actively seek to actualize their full human potential, not only through their most significant relationships, but through the families they create, the careers they pursue and the communities they participate in building. In other words, the kind of education I'm talking about could help countless people not only to rid themselves of addictions, but to get in touch more deeply and intimately with their own humanity.

Sadly, as it stands, global economic competition threatens to thwart our ability to realize the quality of life that all of us might want to have. But if it's hard to find a balanced way of life in the West, imagine how much more difficult it is in nations that are only now undergoing their own industrial revolutions, living with abject poverty, overcrowding and disease in urban slums, and working in conditions that are tantamount to slave labour. Connected to the global village by the Internet, many people in the developing world increasingly express a desire for the same opportunities and choices as their counterparts in the West. A growing number of voices say they want the freedom to choose who they want to be and to choose the person they want to share their lives with, the ability to balance their family and work lives, and the knowledge that the rights of women and children will be valued and protected as much as the rights of men. And I believe this could all grow from the simple step of introducing relationship, self-awareness and love education to our children while they're in school to help them prepare for the most important journey of their lives.

Being in the Now or Becoming the Now

I'd like to close this discussion of true romantic love with some thoughts on the well-known concept of "being in the now." This is indeed a useful idea, especially for people in crisis. A person dealing with severe pain may experience such anxiety that the anxiety increases their pain. Changing their thinking to being in the moment, or being in the "now," can help alleviate that anxiety and reduce the pain. This also holds true for a person who is suicidal, for whom it is far better to focus on getting through each moment than to risk being overwhelmed and giving in to self-destructive impulses. For similar reasons, being in the now can help an addict get through the first agonizing days of recovery.

But at some point, when the darkest moments are over, we have to begin thinking of the future again. This ability to think about and plan for the future is one of the things that distinguishes humans from animals. With a reflective consciousness and emotional capabilities, we seek meaning in life by actualizing our full human potential.

Some spiritual teachers claim that all we have is the now. This appears logical, but it's somewhat incomplete. Actions are intentional, which means, literally, we perform them with intent—and intent, by its nature, is about the future. The future might be five seconds from now, or five months, or fifty years, but the actions we take and the choices we make in the now not only create our possible future, but may also reshape our perception of the past.

Spending time "in the now" through meditation or contemplation can be a positive spiritual practice. Contemplation can quiet the mind, leading to a feeling of greater peace and reduced anxiety. It is possible to connect to the eternality of the universe and our divine essence, which is immortal. This can be a blissful experience, providing a glimpse of the spiritual home from which we came and to which we will return. But I believe that it is not the best state from which to conduct human life.

There are two counterproductive side effects of "being in the now." I'll call the first one *spiritual avoidance*. Here, the goal is to focus only on the moment without thought of the past or the future. This approach is often used to avoid feeling pain from the past. But it can numb us and cause us to avoid thinking about the past in a way that might help us learn. We may live in the present moment, but we must maintain a connection to the past.

It can also be helpful to actively consider the future, as the actions we take and the choices we make now inform and shape our potential. Here's an example. Imagine that in this moment, you and your partner are standing in front of a marriage commissioner, family and friends. You are fully present in the moment to honour your commitment to your partner by citing your marriage vows. Every word you utter affirms your intentions of creating a new life together with your partner. You chose this person as your lifelong partner because of lessons learned from a previous romantic relationship. Your broken heart left you with tremendous self-doubt and fear of attachment. To protect yourself, you chased short-lived relationships and casual dates. You always told your lovers after sex that you were a die-hard fan of living in the moment, which precluded thoughts about the future. Thus, you asked them not to expect anything from you in the future. You lived in a timeless now.

But when you met your partner, your attitude toward love and life changed. Because of them, you began to believe in the future again and you wanted to have as much of your future time together as possible. You began living not only for now but for the years to come. This was the reason you decided to get married. Marriage is a plan for the future. With love, you find the courage to commit to outgrowing the fear that originated in your past. With love, you live fully in the present moment, while also committing to building a future together.

The second potentially negative consequence of being in the now is a sort of nihilism, a belief that life is without intrinsic meaning, purpose or value. This is summed up in the buzzword

"YOLO"—an acronym for "you only live once"—which can be used to justify and excuse all manner of behaviours, especially those involving indulgences or addictions that we seek to anaesthetize our pain. The problem is that those indulgences frequently hurt us and others much more in the long run than if we simply faced up to our pain. In other words, while there is a time and a place for being in the now, the idea and practice are open to abuse.

Depending on your outlook, you may find what I call "becoming the now" to be a more useful concept. I use this phrase as a way of rolling three dimensions in life—the fixed past, the experiential present, and the possible future—into one. Becoming the now gives you a reason to work through the issues that have plagued your past and continue to plague your present so that they might not plague your future. Becoming the now enables divine stillness to shine through your ego-self to liven your life and relationships. Becoming the now gives you a reason to actualize your full human potential in the pursuit of a better you in a better future.

Becoming the now doesn't preclude being in the now, but incorporates and extends it. Becoming the now means you are present in the moment, but aware that this moment will lead to another moment, and another; with understanding that your actions now will affect the future for you and others; with awareness that in each moment of being who you are, you are also becoming who you will be. Where being in the now can become a sort of anaesthetic, a hiding place in which you avoid working toward a better, more enlightened future self, becoming the now is more like a breath of fresh, cool mountain air that awakens your senses to everything that has been, is now, and will be.

Love Is a Journey

In Chapter 1, I defined love as a sacred path, and soulmate relationships as our primary vehicle for spiritual growth. I gave three reasons for this: First, we are driven by a powerful urge to merge with another being. Second, romantic love serves as a universal conduit for spiritual growth. And third, romantic love is a journey of spiritual self-awareness. Returning to the third of these ideas, let me give you an example. Let's imagine that in the past, your relationship efforts have been mainly focused on how you could entice a potential love interest to feel attracted to you. You might have picked up a lot of dating and relationship skills from YouTube, books and seminars. Although you had some successes, you felt something was not right, as you were not entirely content with your experiences.

Say you had six disappointing and brief relationships over ten years as you searched high and low for "the one." Initially, you thought your dissatisfaction was due to your dating partners' shortcomings. Partner A was too jealous. Partner B was too sexually rigid. Partner C was too selfish. Later, you realized that the same nagging thoughts and feelings would enter your consciousness after each breakup, and that these thoughts and feelings were your problem, and yours alone. You wondered what was wrong with you that you would repeatedly create or gravitate toward the same dysfunctional dynamics.

The ongoing unhappiness in your love life has driven you to embark upon a spiritual quest, although you may not have seen it as such when you started out. It is the quest for self-awareness, which is a common ground in almost all schools of spirituality.

To understand yourself better, you redirect your attention inward instead of outward. You turn to relationship experts, therapists and psychologists who teach you how to know yourself better in order to figure out what you really want, and why you want what you want. After deep reflection, you realize that what you need from your partner is for them to be kind, considerate, intelligent and fun to be with. These experts ask you to reflect on why you want these qualities in particular. From this type of self-reflective exercises, you become not only more aware of your own needs and wants, but also other people's behavioural patterns, emotions and thoughts.

You are surprised by how much you have learned about yourself. Yet the real eye opener from this exercise is learning that the person who enables your happiness is not your partner, but yourself. Because of this awareness, you lose interest in dating someone who is either unconscious of their behaviour and needs, or manipulative and exploitative with your needs and emotions. With more self-knowledge of what makes a relationship work harmoniously, you can connect more deeply with your current partner because you know what you want, why you want it and how to communicate better to achieve it. The new way in which you relate to your partner is gradually and reflexively transforming the human qualities that you bring into the relationship. You are going through a profound existential transformation.

FURTHER CONSIDERATION

- Do you engage in any spiritual practices, e.g. meditation, qigong or yoga? In what ways can they help you become a better person?

- Can you recall the three levels of attunement from earlier in the chapter? Can you recall a relationship that featured all three? Would you consider it true romantic love?

- What are the three characteristics of true romantic love? When you think back on your romantic relationships, what examples can you give of each of these characteristics being present in your life? If you can't think of such examples in your own life, try to think of examples you've witnessed in the relationships of friends or family members.

- Have you ever been or are you now in a relationship that started out well but, after a while, you found yourself feeling lonelier and emptier than ever? Why do you think you felt/ feel that way? How did you address or are you addressing this? How much success did you have or are you having? If the relationship is over, how did it end and how do you feel about it now? If you're still in that relationship, what will you do next?

- In what ways do you think true romantic love, as described in this chapter, can help you become a better person? Have you ever had such an experience?

- What do you think of the idea of teaching love and relationship essentials in high school? Would you have been more likely to seek counselling for relationship issues if you'd known at a younger age that they could be caused by problems with your mental and emotional health and that those problems could be alleviated?

- How would you describe the difference between "being in the now" and "becoming the now"? Can you identify times in your life when you've used being in the now as a way to justify unhealthy or avoidant behaviour?

THREE

Falling in Love

FOR CENTURIES, WESTERN philosophers, psychologists, anthropologists and sociologists have tried to explain why we fall in love.

Some theories seek a biological explanation. In her 2004 book *Why We Love*, anthropologist Helen Fisher writes that the feeling we call love is created by three mood-regulating hormones—dopamine, norepinephrine and serotonin—interacting with brain circuitry.[1] This interaction evolved over time, she suggests, because when humans procreated, producing infants that were more helpless and had a longer maturation period than other animals, their offspring required ongoing care from two parents: one to nurture, the other to provide. To support her theory, Fisher teamed up with two radiologists to scan the brain and identify which part was activated when one falls in love. And indeed she found evidence to support her theory.

Yet Fisher's research is flawed in at least one way. There are many social models that could have evolved around the care of children other than the model of a man and a woman coupling up for this purpose alone. In other words, humans do not need to fall in love in order to create two persons bonding to care for offspring.

In his groundbreaking book, *The Structure of Scientific Revolutions,* Thomas Kuhn points out that there is no objective foundation for knowledge, as the discovery of knowledge itself is paradigm-dependent.[2] He points out that if scientists want to practise science, they must commit to adhering to the standards and assumptions set by the scientific community. The philosophical paradigm underpinning science is materialism, which posits that the only thing that exists is physical matter. According to this perspective, human consciousness emerges from physical matter. Therefore, human consciousness ceases to exist once the physical body stops functioning. This philosophy by definition excludes the concept of a soul. The practice of modern science is based on this presupposition, therefore scientists must look for material causes to explain their theories. Consequently, it is no surprise that Dr. Fisher discovers a material (biological) cause to explain romantic love. Since science has replaced the Church as the arbiter of modern-day truth, what we know about love and human nature is distorted by this conjecture without our having any awareness of our own indoctrination.

Most of us are not aware that who we are and what we believe is obscured by the biases of the materialistic philosophy underpinning modern science. But the concept of the soul will only be accepted as truth when a new standard emerges. The philosophy that guides how science is practised must make a paradigm shift from materialistic to spiritual philosophy in order to recognize the concept of soul. I believe this will happen one day.

Although the existence of a soul has yet to be proven by

science, accepting and understanding the soul is the best way to understand many aspects of life, including why humans have the *capacity* to fall in love. And there is a difference between *how* we fall in love and *why* we fall in love.

Fisher's research is based on a materialistic approach to the biology behind the phenomenon. But in a soul-based approach, humans are endowed with the capacity to fall in love as a means for spiritual growth. Our capacity to fall in love moves our souls a step closer, in each lifetime, toward the moral and spiritual maturity all souls strive for.

The various theories of love advanced by contemporary relationship writers, therapists and spiritual teachers often conflict dramatically with each other. This does little more than cultivate confusion and anxiety in those whom they seek to help or teach. Understanding that love is the soul's primary purpose can help dispel that confusion.

It can also serve as a litmus test to help us distinguish true romantic love from its imposters, which I'll define in future chapters.

Love and "Limerence"

Falling in love is a special state of consciousness in which our subjective world is changed instantly and profoundly. This special state is triggered by a defining moment—the moment we experience a romantic spark—when we become aware of a shift in our consciousness. There are different reactions when this spark is ignited, ranging from what feels like a trembling earthquake that turns life upside down, to the peaceful singing of a church choir that feels like bliss. This spark draws us helplessly toward the potential love interest and causes us to long for sexual union with them. This feeling may or may not evolve into a relationship, as it is merely a seed that requires other conditions to grow and bloom.

This special state can enter one's consciousness suddenly or slowly; either way, it comes unexpectedly. The fire can be lit any time from the first moment we lay our eyes on our potential love interest to many years into the relationship. On the other hand, we can know and love a person for our whole lifetime without ever feeling this romantic spark. How long we stay in this special state varies. Some lucky couples never fall out of love, but many of us do. Like falling in love, falling out of love can either be sudden or gradual. However it occurs, it changes us profoundly.

In 1979, Dorothy Tennov published *Love and Limerence*, a landmark book about the nature of romantic love and why we fall in love. In the book, Tennov, an American psychologist, coined the term "limerence" to describe the intense, all-consuming state of heightened romantic interest that marks the beginning of a relationship.[3] Limerence is so intense that it is often identified as infatuation, but there are significant differences.

For one thing, infatuation is based on fantasy and projection, so it burns out quickly upon exposure to the true nature of its object. (We will return to this concept in a later chapter.) But if the desires of the "limerent" are reciprocated by the limerent object (LO), these intense feelings may evolve into true romantic love.

Tennov was a rare love expert who could concisely pinpoint the essence of true romantic love, as summarized by the following twelve components:

· Intrusive thinking about the LO.

· Acute longing for reciprocation.

· Dependency of mood on limerent's interpretation of LO's actions, especially with respect to the probability of reciprocation.

· Inability to react limerently to more than one person at a time (except when limerence is at a low ebb, early in the relationship or as it fades).

- Fleeting and transient relief from unrequited limerent passion through vivid imagination of action by LO, which might mean reciprocation.

- Fear of rejection and sometimes incapacitating but always unsettling shyness in LO's presence, especially in the beginning and whenever uncertainty strikes.

- Intensification through adversity (at least, up to a point).

- Acute sensitivity to any act or thought or condition that can be interpreted favourably, and an extraordinary ability for the limerent to interpret even the most neutral actions on the part of the LO as signs of the LO's hidden passion.

- An aching of the "heart" (a region in the centre front of the chest) when uncertainty is strong.

- Buoyancy (a feeling of walking on air) when reciprocation seems evident.

- A general intensity of feeling that leaves other concerns in the background.

- A remarkable ability to emphasize what is truly admirable in LO and to avoid dwelling on the negative, even to respond with a compassion for the negative and render it, emotionally if not perceptually, into another positive attribute.[4]

Tennov describes how the behaviour of one of her research participants transformed after falling in love: "At the office, I could hardly keep from shouting out how deliriously happy I felt. The work was easy; things that had annoyed me on previous occasions were taken in stride. And I had strong impulses to help others; I virtually sprang to my feet to assist. Mary! My former 'enemy!' No one was an enemy anymore! My affection included the universe. I loved every single creature. A fly landed on my desk, I hadn't the heart to brush it away."[5]

If all of us fell in love like this woman, we would not need the United Nations or religion to uphold peace! The best way to solve international conflicts would be for everyone to fall in love at the same time. And that sums up the beauty of real love—it's not only about feeling good about life and the world, but about its potential to transform the lover into a better person in the presence of the beloved.

The power to transform our egoistic self to a universal self is a component of the reciprocity that is such an essential element of falling in love. It's this desire for reciprocity that endows love with a spiritual dimension. This feeling of reciprocity confuses many thinkers, novelists and relationship experts. When we are truly in love, what we want most is not simply to have sex with our beloved, or to be with this person all the time, or to create a social and material life with the beloved. What we want most is to experience the reciprocity of our spiritual feelings of oneness through the act of tender loving care for our beloved's well-being.

As Tennov suggests, something that so consistently eludes precise definition is often deemed "spiritual." The goal of limerence is not to possess, but to merge, to experience the ecstatic bliss of oneness with the beloved. In fully developed limerence, the limerent also wants the LO to be safe, cared for, happy, and all those other positive and noble feelings that people have for their children, parents and dearest friends. But what the limerent most desires is to have their feelings returned. This is because the essence of true romantic love includes individuation, freedom and equality. As Tennov writes: "a king might own his subject or slave; if he is also in love with her, he might give her freedom so that she can express mutuality 'freely'... The goal of limerence is not possession, but a kind of merging, a 'oneness,' the ecstatic bliss of mutual reciprocation."[6]

Imagine being that king, having absolute power. To your surprise, you fall for a slave girl—and not only a woman of a whole other class, but also of another race. Since you cannot stop thinking of her, you want to honour your feelings. However, because this is true romantic love, you will not use your political power to possess her. Although you can have her body, what you want most is for her to desire you the same way you desire her. Because you've fallen into true romantic love with her, she is no longer an object but an individual.

As king, you grant her freedom so she can choose whom to love, hoping she will choose you of her own free will. But you don't want her to choose you only because you could give her more than she could never imagine. Rather, you want her to love you for who you are. In true romantic love, everyone is equal, including kings and slaves.

If, after freeing her, this slave girl does not return your love, you will be heartbroken. But because of the transformative power of love, you will change the law in your kingdom to free all slaves and facilitate interracial relationships. You will find ways to provide for her and her people. Through your love for her, you will become a better person.

As the saying goes, love is blind. Society has long frowned on romantic love because it can cause us to ignore differences in race, ethnicity and language, or gaps in age, socio-economic status and education. But, as Jesus taught, we practise universal love when our love for another blinds us to these differences.

Crazy, Stupid Love

Is love a form of madness?

The Western, psychology-driven view of limerence is that it is a form of mild psychosis: obsessive, compulsive and delusional.

We see no flaws in the object of our affection. They consume our heart and mind.

Sigmund Freud, whose work has informed Western views of psychology, saw falling in love through the lens of Oedipus and Electra complexes.[7] (An unconscious desire to own the opposite-sex parent and kill the same-sex parent.) Therefore, he saw it as a form of mental illness. M. Scott Peck, author of the 1978 book *The Road Less Traveled*, discounted romantic love as infantile regression.[8] Erich Fromm, author of the 1956 classic *The Art of Loving*, discounted romantic love as beyond rational, logical comprehension[9] Modern psychologists have linked romantic love with obsessive-compulsive disorder, and even identified a specific, love-linked type of the disorder called relationship obsessive-compulsive disorder (ROCD).[10] Indeed, if love is unrequited, the limerent's road to moving on can be long and difficult.

It's understandable that many people, especially academics, consider people who are "in love" to be irrational, not fully mentally balanced. Limerence can blind us not only to differences in race, age, social group, family status, culture and class, but also to personality flaws that, by all objective standards, should render a person a poor relationship prospect.

Yet, the experience can be transformative under the right conditions.

Our family members and friends may tell us we have made a bad choice, yet under the spell of romantic love, we don't want to hear the truth. Romantic love is like a dormant volcano that wakes up in its own time and runs its course, independently of our own will. This powerful eruption of raw energy can make lovers do many silly things they would not normally do to win over their beloved. When we are in this special state, love controls us. We are no longer the same person as our lives are hijacked by the image of our beloved. This experience can be especially frightening for individuals who pride themselves on being rational, sensible and logical.

Even our colloquialisms and clichés reflect the notion that falling in love is a form of temporary insanity: we say we've been "bitten by the love bug" or "struck by Cupid's arrow" as though stricken by disease or injured by a weapon. We say someone is "madly in love," "lovesick" or "head over heels in love." In some instances, the "heat of passion" is even considered a legitimate defence against criminal charges, most often murder triggered by an act of infidelity. The point of a "crime of passion" defence is to show that an accused—a normally sane person—was temporarily out of their mind, and therefore the crime couldn't have been premeditated. This has been known to succeed in reducing the charge from murder to manslaughter, with the result of a much more lenient punishment.[11]

Yet, unlike true forms of insanity, we crave this mysterious experience and spend much of our lives seeking it out, working to preserve it or grieving over the loss of it. When we are in love, we feel we are the lucky ones, as if life is finally worth living. Falling in love wakes us up from the humdrum and gives us reasons to keep moving forward.

Infatuation

Relationship opinion-makers encourage people to build love relationships out of friendships, in a slow, controlled way, and especially encourage people to avoid believing in "love at first sight," which they simply consider infatuation and therefore not love. Many people believe true love takes time—that we can only experience true love if we know the person because true love is built on friendship and knowledge. These thinkers frown on the idea of love at first sight because they believe it is impossible to fall madly in love with someone without knowing them. Consider this advice from Ann Landers in an advice column published in the *Chicago Tribune* titled "Infatuation Or Love?"

Infatuation is fleeting desire—one set of glands calling to another. It is marked by a feeling of insecurity. You are excited and eager but not genuinely happy. There are nagging doubts, unanswered questions, little bits and pieces about the relationship that you would just as soon not examine too closely. It might spoil the dream.

Love is friendship that has caught fire. It takes root and grows, one day at a time. Love is quiet understanding and mature acceptance of imperfection. It is real. It gives you strength and grows beyond you—to bolster your beloved. You are warmed by his presence, even when he is away. Miles do not separate you. You have so many wonderful films in your head that you keep replaying. But near or far, you know he is yours, and you can wait.

Infatuation says, "We must get married right away. I can't risk losing him." Love says, "Be patient. Don't panic. Plan your future with confidence."

Infatuation has an element of sexual excitement. Whenever you are together, you hope it will end in intimacy.

Love is not based on sex. It is the maturation of friendship that makes sex so much sweeter. You must be friends before you can be lovers.

Infatuation lacks confidence. When he's away, you wonder if he's being unfaithful. Sometimes, you check.

Love means trust. You are calm, secure and unthreatened. He feels your trust, and it makes him even more trustworthy.

Infatuation might lead you to do things you will regret, but love never steers you in the wrong direction.

Love is elevating. It lifts you up. It makes you look up. It makes you better than you were before. [12]

According to Landers, love based on friendship is good, but love without any knowledge of the person is bad.

While this may be true for people lacking in emotional maturity—those, for example, whose souls haven't matured from previous lives—I have come across several couples who fell madly in love at first sight and who have remained together for decades. This does not mean these couples don't have relationship challenges; it simply means they didn't need to know their future partner for very long to experience romantic love that resulted in a lifelong bond.

George is well known at the office for being a dedicated carnivore who loves steak, roast beef and hamburgers, and hates vegetables, which he calls "rabbit food." When a cute new guy, David, starts work at the same office, George falls for him. He can't stop thinking about tall, handsome David, and finds himself making excuses to go to his desk to ask him questions or invite him out for drinks after work.

When they go out to lunch one day, David suggests a vegan restaurant. That evening, George vows to give up meat and live as a vegan to be more aligned with David. At one point, David mentions something in passing about animal rights; George joins PETA. His commitment to transforming his life doesn't last long, though. Within two weeks, he's sneaking hamburgers every chance he gets, and backing out on a commitment he'd made to participate in an animal-rights demonstration. George is not in love; he's infatuated, and the infatuation is burning out. He hasn't made deep changes in his life because he wants to be a better person for his beloved; he's made superficial changes that he hopes will catch David's eye so he'll want to sleep with him.

David, meanwhile, has his eye on Peter. His attraction to Peter surprises David; Peter is not vegan, and David never thought he could fall for someone who eats meat. But Peter and David have talked about it, and Peter has as clear a moral reason why he believes eating meat is acceptable as David has why he believes it's wrong. In fact, Peter takes a strong ethical position on almost every aspect of his life, yet he doesn't judge those who don't share his opinions.

David has been almost magnetically drawn to Peter from the moment he laid eyes on him, and the more they get to know each other, the more strongly he feels that this relationship is meant to be. This feeling makes him want to look more closely at his own opinions and beliefs. It's not that he thinks he and Peter need to be aligned in everything they believe—he's not going to give up veganism, and neither does he expect Peter to give up eating meat—but that Peter makes him want to be a better person all around, including relaxing his judgmental attitudes about diet and lifestyle.

THERE IS A saying in the computer industry: "garbage in, garbage out." It means that nonsensical input data will produce nonsensical output data. We don't blame the computer for producing junk, but the person who inputs the data. Similarly, falling in love is a function. There's no point blaming the function for the result if a poor source of input results in poor output. In the case of infatuation, the poor input may be lack of maturity, personality conflicts or previous experiences. But if love at first sight doesn't work out because of these things, it's not love's fault!

Reclaiming "Love at First Sight"

It is not essential to believe in reincarnation to believe in the soul, or the role of the soul in attaining spiritual and moral maturity in this earthly life and beyond it. But when falling in love is viewed through a reincarnation lens, it can explain much about how we know when we've crossed paths with a soulmate. And it can also explain why the result can sometimes be what we call "love at first sight."

In *Journey of Souls,* Michael Newton explains the love-at-first-sight experience that led him to his soulmate:

I was blessed by three specific clues to help me find my wife. Thumbing through *Look* magazine as a teenager, I once saw a Christmas advertisement for Hamilton watches modeled by a beautiful dark haired woman dressed in white. The caption in the ad said. "To Peggy," because she was holding a wrist watch as a gift from an imaginary husband. An odd sensation came over me, and I never forgot the name or face. On my twenty-first birthday I received a watch of the same make from a favourite aunt.

A few years later, while attending a graduate school in Phoenix, I was washing a load of white laundry one Saturday. Suddenly, the first trigger was activated in my mind with the message, "It's time to meet the woman in white." I tried to shake it off, but the face in the ad pushed all other thoughts away. I stopped, looked at my Hamilton watch and heard the command, "Go Now." I thought about who wears white. Acting as if I was obsessed, I went to the largest hospital in the city and asked at the desk for a nurse matching the name and description.

I was told there was such a person who was coming off her shift. When I saw her, I was stunned by the resemblance to the picture in my mind. Our meeting was awkward and embarrassing, but later we sat in the lobby and talked non-stop for four hours as old friends who hadn't seen each other for a while—which, of course, was true. I waited until after we were married to tell my wife about the reason I came to her hospital and the clues given to me to find her. I didn't want her to think I was crazy. It was then I learned that on the day of our first meeting she had told her astonished friends, "I just met the man I'm going to marry."[13]

Signs that we're reconnecting with our soulmates may include: feelings of familiarity, safety and comfort; a sense of déjà vu; and immediately wanting to be pulled into the person's orbit.

The feeling of familiarity is a strong, energetic sensation. It is not exactly a bodily state, but an impression in the consciousness. More than just feeling instantly comfortable with this person, we feel attached to them.

Moreover, the feeling is reciprocal. If one person has a feeling of familiarity but the other person does not, it is not a past-life encounter. Rather, this stranger may represent an important archetype (universal symbol) for a parent, goodness, divinity, beauty or power already embedded in the psyche. It is easy to fall in love with a stranger if they represent unresolved archetypical conflicts we bring with us into the current life. In these cases, our attachment is to the conflicts in our past lives, not to the individual we've just met in this life.

Strangers who project archetypical conflicts onto our awareness are not people with whom we've had actual relationships in past lives. Yet crossing paths with someone who has suffered the same wounds in this life—especially when those wounds have caused us to develop either similar or diametrically opposite ways of dealing with conflict—can create an intense romantic liaison, which can grow into genuine romantic love. This is one way we "grow out of" our current soul group and move on to a more mature soul group.

For example, both Linda and Joseph were abandoned by their parents when they were small. Because of this wound, they were instantly attracted to each other—it was love at first sight. Because of her fear of abandonment, Linda became clingy, always afraid of being left alone. Joseph reacted to the same type of wound in the opposite way; by avoiding feelings of attachment and the abandonment he feared attachment would bring.

These two attachment styles are common among people with

abandonment issues, and became the source of their romantic conflict. Because they wanted to use their relationship to heal, Linda and Joseph worked together to uncover the real cause of their conflict. As Linda tried to be less clingy, Joseph let himself attach to Linda more. The more attached Joseph became, the more secure Linda felt. The more secure Linda felt, the less clingy she became, and the safer Joseph felt about attaching. Their efforts to consciously use each other to heal helped Linda and Joseph develop a deeper and deeper connection with each other.

But even if we feel familiarity and closeness as soon as we meet a soulmate, this feeling may not turn into a romantic attraction. Conditions must be right to transform this feeling of familiarity into romantic love. For example, let's say Irene meets a soulmate who was her brother in a past life. Because of problems in Irene's family in this life, she's never felt cherished or loved as a child should. When she meets her soulmate, she feels an instant connection and sense of security that speaks to her need for familial love in this life. Mistaking it for romantic love, she has sex with him, hoping this will forge a deeper bond between them and fulfill her need for the security of a loving family. But because, in this case, it's only sibling love, Irene's feelings are more infatuation than true romantic love, and this relationship is likely to cause her pain if she demands more of it than it is meant to provide. Irene needs greater emotional maturity to be able to recognize love at first sight if and when it comes along.

To connect with any romantic soulmate, but particularly to experience love at first sight, there must be enough reciprocated romantic attraction to overcome obstacles. Many conditions may prevent two potential romantic soulmates from seeing their connection in this light:

· Lack of psychic awareness. Recognizing a soulmate requires psychic sensitivity. Many people are not attuned to their psychic abilities.

- Unfavourable life circumstances. If a person is distracted by something in their life at that moment, they may not be open to interpreting a connection as romantic.

- An existing relationship. A person may not be open to another relationship at the time they encounter a soulmate because they are already in one.

- Lack of readiness. A person may simply not be ready for a relationship at the time they encounter a soulmate so they may simply ignore this powerful experience.

- Fear. A person is afraid to get involved again if they have not yet dealt with their pain from a previous relationship.

- Cultural conditioning. Because mainstream Western culture and Christianity lack the concept of love at first sight, the Western mind may not recognize a soulmate when they appear.

Let's look at some of these conditions in more depth.

Intuition and Psychic Abilities

We receive information in two ways: through our senses, and through intuition. Both types of input must be "downloaded" into our brains where the information is labelled, identified, processed, interpreted and given meaning. Concepts and cultural beliefs help us understand the sensory and energetic information we receive.

Our intuition (which I equate with psychic ability), plays an important role in guiding our growth and connecting with our soulmate. Many of us are out of touch with this aspect of ourselves, yet it still plays a part in our lives.

How we make sense of our experiences and what meaning we

give them is intimately embedded in our worldview. Moreover, to improve our capacity for romantic love, we need a broader and deeper knowledge of human nature. An important feature of the reincarnation worldview is that humans are energetic beings with psychic potential. These psychic abilities enable us to intuitively connect with the world around us, i.e. in a love-at-first-sight connection. The same psychic capacities that enable us to attune to cosmic and other consciousnesses at an energetic level are also the source of moral feeling and creativity. Our innate psychic capacity allows us to attune and connect to other people's emotions, thus allowing us to experience empathy.

Buddhists believe nothing exists but the mind (consciousness), which can mean the mental content, the thinking process, the conceptual mind, the higher self/soul, our awareness, our non-differentiated consciousness or the cosmic consciousness.[14] The mind and body together are an energy system that can manifest at different levels of vibrational frequency, although the body, due to its material reality, vibrates at a lower frequency than the mind. To those who work to develop their psychic abilities by attending psychic schools or studying with teachers, the vibrational frequency manifests as a visible aura around the body. When the vibration of the body and the mind are in sync, we are able to tap into the cosmic consciousness.

We receive energetic information before sensory information. Our own energy system picks up on another person's energy to create an impression or intuition based on our subconscious reading of that person's aura.

This impression can be positive, neutral or negative. A positive connection results when our own vibrational frequency is similar to or complements the other person's. At other times, for no reason that we can explain, our intuition will make us feel jittery and insecure. Most often, our impression will be neutral.

Although we are all endowed with the potential for psychic ability, most of us must work to cultivate it. The three most common psychic abilities most of us can access through practice are clairvoyance, clairaudience and clairsentience.[15]

"Clair" means clear; indeed, if we are trained properly, the information we receive through these psychic abilities is clearer than sensory information. Clairvoyance is the ability to visualize the occurrence of an event before its time; clairaudience is the ability to hear voices from the spirits in higher dimensions. With clairsentience, a person is able to attune to the emotional vibrational frequency of another person.

I categorize people into three levels of psychic ability: average, highly sensitive (called "empaths" in New Age circles) and psychics. In our culture, which values rational thought more highly than intuition, we tend to lose this ability as we mature physically. Most of us don't want to believe in or are afraid to develop our psychic ability. Thus, we train ourselves to distrust our intuition.

Opening the Heart

I challenge the widespread idea that romantic love, particularly love at first sight, is irrational or pathological. I agree that people can be delusional and some love-at-first-sight experiences are the wishful projections of an unbalanced and unhealthy personality. But it doesn't follow that everyone who experiences these intense feelings is going through a mental-health crisis. From a reincarnation worldview, love at first sight is possible because the couple had a deep connection in their past lives. It can be understood as the beginning of the process of evolution in our consciousness, the transformation of human qualities we call love. This intense instant bonding enables two lovers to refine their capacity for love in this life. In fact, love at first sight can be a great spiritual gift because it temporarily opens the heart wide, blinding us to our lover's human flaws so they shine with the beauty that is actually their true essence.

Seen in this light, the central issue in the concept of love at first sight is not its plausibility but the lens through which we observe and experience the world. The only thing that makes the concept of love at first sight seem ludicrous is the worldview we subscribe to. If we change our worldview, we also change the meaning we make of reality.

If the concept of soulmate as understood from a reincarnation worldview is true, everlasting romance is possible. An unfinished romantic love from a past life can carry forward into the current life or from the current life into future lives.

Many relationship experts caution us against believing in love at first sight because if we dive into love without thinking it through, previous emotional programming may cause us to choose the wrong partner. Yet if we consider human existence from the reincarnation worldview, it's possible we could choose a person with whom we'll have a difficult relationship in this life because we have unfinished business with that person from a previous life, and we will continue to struggle with the same soul until we have learned the necessary karmic lesson from this particular connection.

It's Complicated

In fact, crossing paths with a soulmate may not be a romantic experience at all. Many people claim their current partners are their romantic soulmates because they feel good about themselves around this particular person. Their partners understand them like no one else can. They have the same thoughts, preferences and experiences as their partners. Their partners can finish their sentences. They don't need verbal communication; they know each other's feelings and desires as if they can read each other's minds.

These are all wonderful qualities in a relationship. But the problem with this conception of soulmate is that it only highlights positive experiences. What if a person with low self-esteem meets someone who triggers their feelings of unworthiness? Why would that encounter not be considered a soulmate reunion? These two souls could be bringing forward unfinished issues from previous lives to resolve in this one. That is part of the definition of a soulmate.

Many people see the idea of a romantic soulmate in a solely positive light as a result of their own immaturity. They want to believe meeting one particular person will instantaneously create happiness. In other words, by simply connecting with this person, their life can be magically transformed. Unfortunately for them, inner transformation only happens to those who are willing to work for it. An internal shift in consciousness may be instantaneous, but it requires ample preparation and hard work to realize. If you believe love can magically transform you, you will likely be disappointed. There is a difference between a change in desire, which can take mere moments, and changes in attitudes, habits or qualities, which can take multiple lifetimes. In some soulmate relationships, reconnection with your true romantic soulmates can facilitate this transformative process. Every relationship is a life lesson for which you need to do your homework.

It is also possible that a person that you dislike or even hate was, in a previous life, a romantic soulmate. Conversely, a soul with whom you had a difficult relationship in a previous life could become your sexual/romantic partner in this one. The result could be a codependent relationship due to a carry-over of negative energy. This explains why codependent relationships are notoriously difficult from which to disentangle.

And you may run into more than one romantic soulmate in your current life. Imagine that in the hundred Earth lives you've had, you've travelled with two romantic soulmates in alternating lives. Thus, you had no problem loving one person exclusively. But then in your one-hundred-and-first life, both romantic soulmates travel with you and cross your path one after another. And perhaps one of your soulmates in this life is a man and the other a woman. In this case, it's not only possible that, like Anna in the opening story, you might have equal feelings for two different people at the same time; it's also possible that you would discover you're bisexual in this life. Embracing a different sexuality may be one of your life lessons this time around.

"I Love You, but I'm Not 'In Love' With You"

Sometimes the person you thought was your soulmate turns out not to have been, after all. In the West, we consider it our God-given right to marry whom we love. Yet, one of the most common excuses people use to justify divorce is, "I still love you but I am no longer 'in love' with you." There is a difference between loving and being in love. If you have never fallen in love, it may be difficult to distinguish between these two different states.

If you decide to create a relationship with someone, it is likely there is some level of attraction involved. The strength of the attraction varies depending on the level of desire. When we have a mild interest in a person, we say we like them, which means we enjoy certain qualities about them. But "love" is different from "like." For example, we might love one person because they are physically attractive, another because they have an amazing sense of humour and a third because of their smile or charm. In addition, we might love a fourth person because they are a great cook or they take care of us, and a fifth because we think they would make a great parent or provider. If we replace the word "love" in the above statements with the word "like," the nature of our feelings for each person is completely different.

If we claim to love a person, meaning we love the whole person as they are, but in fact we really only like them for certain qualities that bring us pleasure while other qualities annoy us, we can find ourselves in a relationship with one person while our hearts and eyes are searching for another catch. Invariably, we never find satisfaction because one person can never satisfy all our desires at once, or continue to satisfy our desires as they change over time. If we say we love a person when we really only like them, we can have multiple beloveds (or belikeds!) at the same time. If we enter a long-term relationship because the person has qualities we like that satisfy certain needs rather than because we truly love them, we may, over the course of the relationship, develop strong bonds of affection with them, which we describe as love. We can honestly tell ourselves we are happy in the relationship and love our partners, yet still feel something is missing. Although we dearly love our current partner, we know this person cannot touch our souls. If we've never experienced falling in love, we may not know what's missing, or why we feel lonely and empty—perhaps even as if we are dying inside.

This painful state is even harder to bear if we entered the relationship because there was mutual romantic love, but later in the relationship we fell out of love. Even though a feeling of love endures, we want out because the friendship, affection, common interests or shared history that remain are not enough to mend our pains. Because we have experienced falling in love, we know there is a difference between loving and being in love, and the absence of that in-love feeling is excruciating.

Another difference between loving a person and being in love with them is that, even though we feel close to the person we love, that feeling does not close the spiritual and psychological space between us. Psychologically, loving someone means we are close to them, we feel safe with them, we trust them, yet we know they are distinct and separate entities. For example, it's possible to reach orgasm with a sex partner we like or love without being in love with them. Our physical closeness does not make us feel at one with them, whereas when we fall in true romantic love, it feels different. When we fall in love we fall into oneness with our partner. The psychological and spiritual gap between us closes and we experience a state of union with our beloved. We feel fused with our beloved. They are part of our consciousness and we are part of theirs. They are always on our mind, our consciousness hijacked by their image.

There is another important difference between loving and being in love. A real romantic spark does not happen by choice, but by chance. We can make a conscious choice to love another person, to focus on their positive traits and minimize their negative ones, and generally to behave lovingly toward them. But this is an act of will; it requires effort. In contrast, there is no choice involved in falling in love. Not only does it require no effort, but it would be a significant effort not to behave lovingly toward our beloved. Whereas love is a choice and a decision, falling in love simply happens, and carries us away in bliss.

Intention, Attention and Concentration

Whether you feel a spark the moment you lay eyes on someone or not until much later, it's important to understand the concepts of intention, attention and concentration, and how they bear on the experience of falling in love. When I was studying various types of Chinese martial arts, my teacher instructed us to punch with our minds and project the punch beyond our opponent's body. How far my punch went, and how strongly it was felt by my opponent, would depend on my intention, attention and concentration.

If my intention was to push through my opponent's body, I would pack more energy into my punch. If my attention was focused on the task at hand, my punch would be stronger and more accurate than if my mind was focused elsewhere. If my concentration remained focused on my opponent, my attention would not wander and my intention would remain pure. Meditation is another way to practise these three skills. If we set a clear intention when we sit down to meditate, the experience is likely to have a more powerful and directed effect on our consciousness.

Meditation itself is the practice of paying attention; if we could pay as close attention to everything we do in our daily lives as we do in meditation, life itself would be meditation. Meditation forces us to apply concentration to each moment; that concentration is the essence of meditation.

Falling in love is a psychic state that is underpinned by these three mental capacities. It causes us to attune to and connect with another person's energetic state. (I'll discuss empathic attunement and connection in Chapter 8.) When we fall in love, our higher self, the soul, temporarily fixates on the image of the beloved. We involuntarily experience the states of intention (the desire to be closer to our lover), attention (being observant of their wants and needs), and concentration (focusing on them).

Falling in love is a special state of consciousness. How we maintain this state so that we don't fall out of love becomes a spiritual practice. The quality of each romantic experience depends on the individual's intention, attention and concentration. The purer these are, the easier it becomes for two lovers to connect and merge.

FURTHER CONSIDERATION

- Give examples of how what you say, think and feel is shaped by the knowledge produced by materialistic science. Give examples of the way it's not. Which do you think is more dominant in your life?

- In which areas—faith, love, desire—are your beliefs divided between a spiritual and scientific worldview? How do you reconcile the dichotomy?

- The text suggests humans are endowed with the capacity to love as a means to spiritual growth. Do you agree? If not, why not? Why do you think humans have the capacity to love?

- Have you ever experienced love at first sight? If so, would you describe this experience as more like temporary madness or joyful connection? If you haven't experienced love at first sight, do you think it's possible? Why or why not?

- Do you believe in psychic abilities? Can you remember an instance when a strong impression of someone, positive or negative, turned out to be true?

- At what times in your life has falling in love blinded you to differences between you and your partner in positive ways? At what times has it blinded you in negative ways?

- What are typical signs of liking someone, loving someone and being in love with someone? How do you recognize these signs in someone for whom you have romantic feelings, or in yourself, compared with how you recognize them in someone else?

- How would you describe the difference between becoming infatuated and falling in true romantic love? Can you recall a time in your life when you mistook infatuation for love?

- Have you ever experienced a romantic relationship without love? What was that like for you? What were the pros and cons? Are you still in that relationship? If not, would you ever want such a relationship again?

- What do we mean when we talk about intention, attention and concentration? What do these three elements contribute to true romantic love?

FOUR

Where We Go Wrong: True Love's Imposters

*Check out this can't-miss potential lifetime employment oppor-
tunity! This is a demanding job requiring your attention 24/7.
You must be multi-talented to take care of both my business
and my personal life. You must also be a good entertainer with
strong interpersonal skills to please everyone in my family
including my nagging and narcissistic father. You must be able
to think on your feet, although I will make all the tough deci-
sions, especially the financial ones. You must be capable of
generating enough cash flow to cover your own wages every
month. You must be equipped with adequate strength and
stamina, especially certain parts of your body, as the work can
be physically demanding. You must have movie-star looks and
conform to popular aesthetic ideals. Because the job requires
that you take care of my domestic life, the abilities to cook and*

clean are essential, as are strong language skills and sexual availability on demand. There is no sick leave and no pension plan, but occasionally we'll have some good laughs. There is no job security, as the employment contract can be terminated unilaterally if the performance fails to meet my expectations. I reserve the right to change these expectations arbitrarily and without notice. If you meet these requirements, you could be my future spouse! Submit your relationship CV, along with a cover letter detailing your prior relationship history and at least three references, to the dating website listed in this ad. Please be advised I will check references before selecting candidates to interview.

BE HONEST: HAS your search for a relationship become like a job hunt? If so, you may be experiencing what I call *relationship employment.*

When I was writing this book, a woman I know told me about an experience she'd had with a psychiatrist many years earlier. In her early twenties, she'd gone through a series of short-lived and unhappy relationships. The psychiatrist told her that if she wanted to meet the right man, she needed to make a checklist of traits she wanted in the man with whom she wanted to build a life, and keep looking until she found Mr. Right.

Have you ever been counselled, or attended a relationship workshop, and been told to prepare a compatibility checklist? Is your checklist anything like the list above, though perhaps less detailed? The purpose of this checklist is to outline what you expect from your potential love interest. With this checklist in your heart, perhaps you have signed up with an online dating site. Anyone who's used an online dating service knows how similar these dates can be to a job interview.

If you are not too demanding, and if your compatibility checklist is not 10 pages long, you should able to avoid the sharks in the sea of love and find plenty of beautiful, gentle dolphins as you move from one dating website to the next. If you're reasonably marketable, you should be in a relationship within months after a breakup.

But does that mean you've found true romantic love?

Relationship Employment

Life has a practical side that we need to take care of for ourselves once we reach adulthood: we need to make a living. Some want to work for others and some want others to work for them. Thus, we are in the job market to look for an employer or employee. If we want to work for others and if the remuneration is commensurate with our training, experience and work effort, we continue to honour the employment contract. If the perceived value of remuneration does not justify our work effort, we move on. When we are happy in our job, we stay; if we are not happy, we find another employer. But even if we like our current employer, when a prospective employer offers us something we cannot refuse, we'd be foolish to stay with the current employer out of loyalty. It is a business; no hard feelings. We need to work to survive and enjoy life.

Just as we need to put food on the table, we also have other needs. The more we cannot meet them on our own, the more urgently we search for someone to meet them for us. When people say they are looking for love, what they often mean is they are looking for someone to meet their needs. With this mindset, it should be no surprise when our attitudes toward relationships begin to resemble our attitudes toward employment.

If your search for a relationship, or if the relationship you're in, feels like work, you may not have found true romantic love but rather relationship employment. Say you find a relationship applicant on a dating website devoted to people who want uncomplicated sex. After a few dates, you meet your friends for coffee and tell them you are happy in the relationship as your new partner delivers exactly what you desire. After several back-to-back breakups over the last five years that have driven you to despair, this new relationship is refreshingly uncomplicated. Not only is your partner the best relationship employee you've had so far, but they're so eager to please that they make you feel great about yourself. You quickly come to feel almost as protective toward them as if they were family.

Yet something is missing. You want to believe love is more than this. It's different from any other relationship you've had, but you're still frustrated with it. One day, you go for a long walk alone in the park and shout aloud to the sky, "I want more than this. I want to fall in love. God, please tell me, how do I find the romantic spark that will turn this relationship/job into a lifetime project? I'm so tired of moving from one relationship/job to another."

What you're really asking for is a fast-track formula to foster romantic love in an existing relationship. I don't pretend to know such a magical formula. There are many workshops, books and videos that claim to teach us how to create love, but they are really talking about creating relationships. True romantic love must be spontaneous. This doesn't mean we can't create conditions for a romantic spark to light the fire of lifelong passion in an existing relationship, and we'll talk about that in Chapters 8 and 9. But the truth about true romantic love is that we stumble into it. Either it's there waiting to be discovered, or it isn't.

On occasion, maybe our relationship evokes such feelings of pleasure, contentment, satisfaction and deep attachment at having our physical, material, sexual, financial, social and psychological needs and wants met that we feel it is love. When this occurs, I call it *relationship-employment love*. It's rare, but if it feels like love and makes both partners happy, who am I to criticize? But if relationship-employment love meets all our needs and yet it still feels like something is missing, maybe it's because it's not true romantic love.

Mind, Heart and Soul

In this chapter, I use three words to talk about love: mind, heart and soul. The mind is the source of thought and intellect, which can induce feelings, including those related to our hearts. And from the Chinese perspective, heart and mind are one. As the heart is the source of emotions and desires, which in turn induce thoughts, a synergy between the mind/reason and the heart/ feeling can lead to relationship-employment love. But true romantic love comes from the soul. Although it can also induce feelings relatable to the heart, it involves mind, heart *and* soul, and the power of the soul trumps the feelings induced by mind and heart alone.

Many of us read a myriad of relationship self-help books, or attend workshops to improve our relationship skills. But learning new skills does not necessarily help us with our humanistic growth. Instead, these new skills are usually about problem-solving. We are unhappy in our relationship, so we need to learn new skills to become happy in our relationship. If there is demand, there will be supply. This is how two industries, the relationship self-help industry and the spirituality self-help industry, have flourished since the 1970s. Both, coming from different angles, focus on finding love. It is a popular trend in the West to turn to New Age spirituality to solve relationship problems. Consequently, some spiritual and relationship gurus bundle spirituality together with love, sex and relationships and teach personal- and spiritual-development workshops.

This is the problem with some aspects of the relationship self-help industry. If you want to find a relationship and are taught new skills to find relationship employment, you will achieve your goal. However, if you want to find love but you are taught instead how to find a relationship, you are bound to have an empty heart.

These programs are not about changing our human qualities. They exist so we can learn new ways to satisfy our endless desire for pleasure. This is why the concept of effortless abundance is understandably appealing to some New Age believers. We want pleasure; we don't want pain. Some relationship experts and spiritual teachers persuade love consumers to create a version of love that is nothing more than pleasure derived from satisfying our needs. To these experts, relationships and love are synonymous.

Because there are so many people in this world wanting love relationships, these offerings have become a multi-billion-dollar industry. This may seem innocent enough—business is business—but when their version of love leaves us feeling empty and constantly seeking new ways to generate feelings of pleasure, our seeking may turn into relationship addiction. We may move from one dating website to another, one partner to another, always seeking the high of a new relationship, never knowing how to find love that will last, perhaps never even understanding that a different and better version of love exists. That can lead to a lot of very unhappy people who feel lonely down to their souls.

Don't get me wrong: I'm not anti-learning. Relationship skills are important to improving the quality of any relationship. Aside from that, there's a lot of joy to be derived from learning new skills and creating new experiences with them. The challenge is not with learning new skills, but with why you want to learn them. If you go to a workshop or see a therapist or read a book to learn new relationship skills, what is your intent? Do you want to be a better human being, or do you simply want to satisfy your desires and avoid pain? If your motivation to learn relationship skills is simply to get something you want, you're not using your relationship to grow as a human—which, not coincidentally, often involves some pain!

It makes sense to learn and use those relationship skills to secure the best relationship employment if you view your lover as a candidate who is meeting your list of needs. But the most rudimentary issue in a relationship is that we forget we are human, as are the people around us. Do you really need to learn relationship skills if the most important thing you need to know to find love is to be human, and to be yourself? This is still a tall order, because being yourself creates a lot of relationship problems, and skills can help with those. But they tend to be more manageable problems because they're related to human fallibility, rather than stemming from the feeling that some unidentifiable thing is just missing—and often blaming your partner for it.

Another thing some relationship experts teach is how to find good relationship employers or employees, and how to avoid poor candidates. In other words, they teach how to identify the candidate with the best experiences, skills and personal traits to meet your relationship-employment needs. Assuming that experts are confusing love with relationships, how can they teach their students to find love? How can they help anyone learn to make a relationship last if their instructions include viewing relationships as jobs and partners as objects, rather than seeing people as human and understanding that what people want most is not just relationships, but love?

Love and relationship have two distinct meanings in this book. Because love is within oneself, to find love you have to look within first. If you are looking for a relationship, your attention is outward first. Not all relationship experts recognize or teach this distinction, though some offer insights about why their students have relationship or love challenges. They point their students in the right direction to find love. Here are four questions to assist you in evaluating whether a particular expert's approach will help you find true love:

· Do these teachers help you to know yourself more deeply?

· Do they direct your attention outward to find the object of your "love," or inward to understand yourself?

- Do they teach you how to be a better human so that you can relate to yourself and others in an authentic and genuine manner?

- Do they guide you to recognize the difference between love and relationships?

When relationship employment evokes such deep feelings of pleasure, satisfaction and attachment that it feels like love, it can last. But most such relationships don't last—or if they do, they don't remain happy. As time goes on, the partners increasingly go through the motions of their relationship. They wonder if life would be better outside of their relationship. They become trapped in their relationship by financial dependency or failing health or other factors. Resentment grows. Eventually, people can find themselves approaching a fifty-year anniversary with no reason to celebrate.

True romantic love, on the other hand, can be a tool that helps you evolve your egoistic self toward your universal self, accelerating your spiritual growth. As spirituality elicits awareness, you know you're in true romantic love if it is helping you see yourself and your life more clearly. Or you can embark on a relationship thinking it's love, but wind up deeply disappointed because you expected so much more. The problem, however, may not have been that you expected too much, but that you were focused on the wrong goal.

Transactional, Conditional and Ego-Driven Relationships

As we've established, a love relationship almost always begins with attraction. You are attracted to someone, and you begin dating. This gives you an opportunity to get to know one another, to find out whether this person meets your needs, and if you can build a relationship with them. If your dates go well, you start seeing each other more, which eventually results in a steady relationship. But that's where the problem arises.

Many people have no problem finding dates but endless problems sustaining a relationship. There are several possible reasons for this, but before we explore them, let's recap the meaning of true romantic love.

True romantic love motivates a lover to want to become a better person. This desire can arise instantaneously or grow gradually. But this transformative power needs a context, i.e. a relationship. The quality of the relationship reflects the qualities and level of maturity of the partners.

In the West, a relationship is usually a set of social arrangements created by two persons. You attract someone because of your interests, needs and wants. You think this potential love interest can satisfy your unique needs and desires. The relationship is a partnership through which the couple works to achieve common goals—and that they be common is crucial. If you need to have fun by travelling alone all over the world, your partner's primary need for the psychological comfort and social support of staying in one place will not be compatible. Similarly, if you want a family and your partner is career-driven, you may have difficulty building a relationship.

At the same time, in the desire to satisfy each other's needs, the relationship is transactional. You must give something up in order to receive something in return. When relationships are transactional, they are also conditional. The length and quality of the relationship is determined by the satisfaction felt by each person in the relationship.

Conflicting needs can create problems, and these problems may be confusing at a spiritual level. Christianity teaches us that *agape* (brotherly love) should be selfless—if we truly love our partners, we should love them regardless of whether or not they meet our personal needs. If we become dissatisfied because our needs aren't being met, does that mean we're not trying hard enough to be a compassionate person who is capable of loving unconditionally? This self-questioning inevitably takes a toll on self-esteem.

But it shouldn't. There's nothing wrong with acknowledging that our needs and desires are not being met. If what two people have together is true romantic love, what they want most— apart from wanting their feelings to be reciprocated—is to be together. The strength of this desire prompts them to seek optimal confliction resolution. True romantic love often brings together people with common and compatible goals, but it can also accommodate lovers with very different goals, because it endows them with the power to grow their identities in the presence of their beloved. Often, this means finding creative ways to compromise. In such cases, learning to sacrifice and compromise in the name of love may be the lesson two people are meant to learn in this life.

One of the potential problems in any transactional, conditional relationship is the presence of power struggles. In the West, we like to believe people in a love relationship should have equal power. There are two challenges with this. First, the distribution of power depends on the stage of development of the two people in the relationship. If partners are at an earlier stage in their development, it is likely one person will dominate, creating rules that favour them. Second, although theoretically any two people at any stage of development can experience true romantic love, it's far more likely to be experienced by people with greater emotional maturity. If one or both lovers have come from dysfunctional situations and bring negative qualities into the relationship, they're going to have a lot of unmet needs, which will make it difficult for them to act maturely toward their partner. They simply may not have the motivation to grow that is required to create a true romantic love relationship. I will talk more about these stages of development later.

So how can you know whether you're experiencing true romantic love or relationship-employment love? For one thing, true romantic love humbles the lovers' pride and need to control. Sharing power is crucial for a healthy relationship. If one person dominates, eventually the other is going to feel their needs are not being met, and that what they thought was true romantic love is not. Disappointment and disillusionment will set in, and one of several things might happen. The one who is not getting their needs met might begin to lose self-esteem. The other partner may become increasingly dominant, and the relationship may deteriorate from there. Or, the one whose needs are unmet will demand more, and the power balance will shift the other way. Or the balance of power in the relationship will bounce back and forth between one extreme to the other, until someone finally says "Enough!" and walks away.

Problems like these can be avoided through a match in maturity levels, and through sustained, heartfelt communication. It opens your vulnerability to your partner, and invites your partner to see who you truly are, without fear. A relationship cannot exist without communication. It is an interactive process in which how you feel, think and behave affects your partner and your partner's response affects you in return. This process is a type of call-response communication by which a couple creates psychological closeness and intimacy. (The concept of call and response will be explained in Chapter 8.) There are different forms of communication between partners in a couple. The highest form is non-verbal intuitive knowledge of each other's state. This happens naturally in true romantic-love relationships in which partners get to know one another very well. By contrast, couples in relationship-employment love are less likely to read each other insightfully, and more likely to resort to superficial forms of communication.

Respecting the Rules

All couples create their own rules in relationships. Rules set boundaries, constraints, and responsibilities. They help regulate behaviour and prevent misunderstandings. They define the role of each person in the relationship, and the nature of the relationship itself.

These rules might be as simple as agreeing to not go to bed angry with each other, or to discuss issues of jealousy as they come up rather than letting them fester. The rules may be as mundane as who does the grocery shopping, or as complex as how to navigate an open relationship.

For a relationship to work, both parties must, at a minimum, agree to uphold whatever rules have been put in place, and to have a system for dealing with broken rules. If disagreements about the rules arise too often, or if one or the other simply ignores the rules, the cracks in their relationship will begin to show. After all, true romantic love not only opens our hearts to our partners, it also makes us adaptable and flexible. If one partner tells the other, "No, I can't live with that," the other partner should respect that. Neither partner would make a change in the rules without mutual agreement.

Of course, not everyone is prepared to make the sacrifices required by a relationship and the rules that go along with it. Some people may feel that they don't want to sacrifice their freedom for the negotiation and compromise required to be with a partner. But it's important to keep in mind that there is no such thing as absolute freedom.

True freedom only exists—only *can* exist—within constraints. Returning to Tennov's story of the king and the slave girl in Chapter 3, the king can only have absolute freedom in his life if he deprives the slave girl of hers. No one can have absolute freedom without depriving others of theirs. Perhaps the largest-scale example of this is democracy, which is based on the understanding that in order for all people to have optimal freedom, they must all agree to live within certain constraints, such as not taking things that belong to others. As long as everyone agrees to live within the same constraints, everyone (theoretically, at least) enjoys the same freedoms.

Like democracy, true romantic love is based on rules, morality, ethics and even empathy. It is both a power and a process. It enables us to learn how to love unconditionally while living within the mutually agreed-upon conditions of the relationship. From this perspective, it's not hard to understand that there is no such thing as absolute freedom, and that any self-sacrifice you make comes back to you a thousand-fold in the love you receive.

True romantic love is about awakening. When you are in true romantic love, you wake up to who you are and what life is about. This awareness is then embodied in the rules you co-create, sustain and evolve with your partner to give identity and life to the relationship.

The Role of Shared Morality

How important are shared moral values? Many people ask relationship experts if they should pair up with someone whose personality is similar or complementary to theirs. Either choice has pros and cons. The important point is that making a long-term relationship work is not a function of personality types but of the qualities two people bring to the relationship, the goals and values they share, and particularly the intertwining of their hearts. All long-term relationships will have friction and disagreements if both partners have strong personalities and if at least some of their life goals, needs and wants differ—as, with two strong personalities, they are bound to do.

As discussed, a relationship is a set of ruled-based social arrangements to facilitate the achievement of common goals set by a couple. Two parties enter a relationship with an understanding that both will honour the rules and take responsibility in creating a fair and equitable exchange according to the rules they agree on, both implicitly and explicitly. What makes a rule-based arrangement work is the moral and ethical beliefs of the partners. These moral and ethical qualities embody love.

Morality is crucial to honouring relationship rules. Whether you are spiritual or not, every relationship has an element of morality and justice, meaning you treat others the way you want to be treated (or you don't treat them in ways you don't want to be treated). If you disregard this fundamental moral principle, the relationship will fail in the long run.

So before asking whether a relationship will work, you must ask whether both partners in the relationship possess the moral qualities of respect, equality, justice, fairness, courage, tenacity, care and other virtues. This is much more important to the longevity of a relationship than compatibility of lifestyle preferences, or even shared goals.

Every relationship has a moral component. True romantic love has the power to bring out the best moral qualities in the lover and the beloved. This empathic power makes the "I" want to evolve into an "us." It endows you with a strong desire to do good, especially to your beloved, because your beloved is part of "us." Your partner's welfare and best interests become your welfare and best interests.

Phantom Romantic Love

Manuel remained single for more than a year after his last girlfriend Suzanne had left him. She had told him that she didn't want him anymore, and that he was a poor boyfriend who always flirted with other girls and had no ambition. Her comments had stung. But, as a result, Manuel decided that in his next relationship he would be the best boyfriend he could possibly be.

One day, Manuel went to the local supermarket to buy groceries. Slipping on a wet floor, he accidentally knocked down a woman in one of the aisles. With embarrassment, he extended his hand to pull the woman up and was struck by the beauty of her eyes. He could not breathe and slipped again, falling to the floor. When the woman laughed and asked why he'd fallen, Manuel gathered up his courage and said, "You have the most beautiful eyes I've ever seen." Manuel was attracted to Debbie from the first moment he saw her, and she picked up on it. She also felt something she could not put her finger on; she had a sense of closeness and familiarity with Manuel, almost as if they were meant to be together. After they met, Manuel thought of Debbie 24 hours a day. Likewise, Debbie wanted to consume all Manuel's energy and time. She would become jealous if Manuel talked to other women. They soon began to spend all their time together.

Their relationship developed quickly because Manuel treated Debbie with respect and gave her plenty of attention. He did everything he could to please her, using the words of love he knew she needed to hear. This made Debbie feel worthy of love. Since the age of six, she had dreamed that one day there would be a Prince Charming to adore her. After 30 years of failed relationships, finally she had found her knight. On many occasions, she told him how envious her friends were, that they all said she had found the best boyfriend. Her compliment made Manuel feel good; he loved playing this role.

And yet now, one year into his relationship with Debbie, Manuel has begun to feel dissatisfied. He feels as though Debbie is allowed to be completely herself in the Goddess role, but he doesn't have that privilege. They argue over small mistakes he makes; he often feels like he can't do anything right. It was as though the minute he let down his guard and stopped playing the role of Prince Charming, she grew critical of him. Bored and frustrated, Manuel returns to his old self. When Debbie is not around, he flirts with every woman available. He does not think of his or their future anymore. He merely wants *to be in the present moment to seek pleasure. Now both Manuel and Debbie cannot stand each other and wonder where the love they once felt for each other has gone.*

IN THE SECTION "Love and 'Limerence,'" in Chapter 3, I introduced Dr. Tennov's research. In her book, she points out a number of traits that characterize falling in love, but does not take her research further to contrast the positive and negative effects caused by this special state of consciousness. Based on Dr. Tennov's definition, you might agree that Manuel and Debbie have fallen in love with each other. However, the question is: Are they in true romantic love? The answer is no. Both Manuel and Debbie are experiencing what I call phantom romantic love, which differs in its motivation, essence and content from true romantic love.

The core of true romantic love is that it motivates a lover to become a better person in the presence of the beloved. This romantic spark not only changes a lover's state of consciousness, but also connects their experiential self with the essence of their soul. It empowers lovers to be who they are in the relationship. Lovers feel free because they are not bound by the roles they play. More, true romantic love enables the lovers to see much more clearly, enabling lovers to change themselves, accept the flaws of a beloved and adapt to life changes.

The enjoyment derived from playing a role in phantom romantic love is profoundly different from the freedom enjoyed within true romantic love. Unlike true romantic love, which is based on connection, the romantic spark in phantom romantic love triggers unmet yearning, unfinished business, a projection of a disowned self onto the object of love. Phantom romantic love does not have power to bring out the essence of the lover's soul; instead this illusory power evokes the past wound or the yearning for the ideal self. Phantom romantic love is a fantasy embedded in a fairytale land that exists in lovers' mind but that lovers attempt to enact in their present physical reality.

Phantom romantic love is also marked by obsession and compulsiveness. Manuel is crazy about Debbie, and that limerence nurtures a delusional image of Debbie. The power of his obsession blinds him to her flaws, and vice versa. They both lack the self-awareness necessary to experience true romantic love, and are stuck at a codependent stage of development.

Manuel's phantom reality, for example, is the re-enactment of his past wounds and the ideal person he wants to be. He unconsciously wants to mend his past wrongs with Suzanne through his relationship with Debbie. The ideal self he wants to be is "the best boyfriend." He sees Debbie as an object in his new love script, and his love for her is motivated by the role he wants to play, not from the essence of his soul. The initial blissful state Manuel and Debbie experience together is owing to their complementary phantom realities: Manuel wants to be Prince Charming and Debbie wants to be worshipped by Prince Charming.

This explains why Manuel feels imprisoned when he wants to experience who he truly is outside this role. And why Debbie would not approve of him stepping outside the role they have created together. Passion fizzles because the images Manuel and Debbie ascribe to one another do not align with their souls. Passion further subsides because Manuel's effort is not constantly rewarded. His sense of inadequacy initial motivates to play the "good boyfriend" role, but only feels good about himself when he gets approval from his Goddess. Ultimately, his passion for Debbie dies when he realizes the gap that exists between his phantom Debbie and the real Debbie.

Some people may confuse falling in love with the concept of a soulmate. There are two possible experiences of falling in love, true or phantom. The object of love can be a romantic soulmate, a non-romantic soulmate or a new soul—someone whose path you are crossing for the first time. In this chapter, I also differentiate between relationship employment and relationship-employment love. There are many permutations of relationships that may look or feel like true romantic love, but are not the real thing.

Thus, phantom romantic love may or may not involve a soulmate. In each lifetime, only a few people will have the capacity to ignite your life passion and make you feel free enough to be your higher self. Without inspiration in the presence of your beloved, phantom romantic love, even with a soulmate, lacks the power to transform the individual—in particular, to turn sexual passion into life passion. You may indeed have fallen in love with a soulmate or romantic soulmate, but perhaps not the right soulmate, not the right person to bring out your zest for life. We'll discuss the differences between and roles of sexual passion and life passion more in Chapter 5.

The Shadow Side of Phantom Romantic Love

Aside from the built-in impermanence of phantom romantic love, one might rightly wonder why there is anything wrong with two people living in a fairy tale, even if only for a while. Life can be hard, after all. Why shouldn't two people find refuge in a dream? Yes, they'll have to come back to reality eventually, but won't the dream have been worth it?

Unfortunately, no. Carl Jung, one of the twentieth century's preeminent thinkers, is credited with having said, "The brighter the light, the darker the shadow."[1] In other words, all of us embody both good and bad traits. When we try too hard to focus on our positive traits, our shadow side—that is, our collection of shortcomings—is suppressed and ignored. As a result, these shortcomings don't improve, and may even get worse.

The nature of phantom romantic love is that at least one of the lovers is pretending to be a more virtuous person than they are. The key word here is "pretending"; if the person were striving, that would imply that they're working hard to be a better person in the relationship, which is a mark of true romantic love. "Pretending" means they want people to believe they're better people than they are without doing the deep emotional work required to get to a better place. Suppressing one's shadow side also makes it more likely that, in one way or another, it will grow in power. This unchecked force can be massively destructive and can harm not only the lover, but also the beloved.

Fairy Tales Are Not Harmless

Elizabeth and Jason are a couple who met as co-workers. The first time Elizabeth saw Jason, she couldn't believe her good fortune. He was the one! After getting to know each other for a while at work, they began dating and within a few years they were married. After years of unhappy relationships, Elizabeth was sure she'd found true love. They had children. Their children grew up. Eventually they celebrated 25 years together. Yet in the 25 years of their marriage, Elizabeth never really felt she deserved Jason. She was very aware of her shadow side, which included terrible rages that she always regretted, but Jason didn't seem to have a shadow side. On top of that, he cared for her when she had health problems, which became increasingly frequent with the passage of time.

Not long after their twenty-fifth anniversary, Elizabeth learned that Jason had been involved in a serious crime in his young adulthood, which he had never disclosed to her. At first, she could rationalize it—he had suffered through a traumatic childhood. And she accepted his explanation that, although he'd never taken legal responsibility for his crime, he'd spent his life trying to be a good person to make up for what he'd done. Eventually, though, Elizabeth realized the thing that hurt her most was Jason's dishonesty. After trusting him with the worst aspects of herself, he'd never trusted her with his. After all the hours she'd spent in counselling for her issues, he'd never sought help for his own. She thought about how much they'd seemed like soulmates in the beginning but how, after a while, he'd started letting things show through about himself that she didn't like. She'd kept telling herself he was perfect, that she herself was deeply flawed, and that she was lucky to have found someone who would put up with her. She told herself that she just needed to work harder at accepting him and their life as it was.

But in the last few years before Elizabeth found out about Jason's past, she'd begun to feel their life and relationship had changed so much since the beginning that she didn't know who she was anymore, and she didn't feel like she knew Jason, either. The changes, she realized, had happened so gradually that she'd just adapted to them. She'd realized that Jason didn't really share her love of travelling as he'd originally said he did, so they didn't travel. She'd realized that he wasn't really interested in any of her social-justice causes, so she stopped talking about them and then she stopped participating in them. She also realized that he'd increasingly been doing things that hurt her, like interrupting her when she was talking about something she was passionate about and changing the subject to something that interested him more. And because Elizabeth had always felt that Jason was a better person than she was, because Jason always talked about their relationship as if they were a perfect prince and princess living a perfect fairy-tale life, she'd stayed with him and changed herself to suit him, until their life had become something she'd never aspired to.

Now, after learning the truth about Jason, Elizabeth began to feel like their life together had been built on lies. She felt devastated, betrayed. She tried to talk to him about it many times, but he didn't really seem to get it. They tried marital counselling, but somehow they always ended up talking about her problems, never his. In desperation, she left him, hoping this would make him understand how unhappy she was and wake him up to the fact that he needed to put effort into their marriage, too. Instead, he quickly moved on to another relationship, replacing Elizabeth with a much younger woman with a personality similar to Elizabeth's 25 years earlier.

Feeling even more devastated, Elizabeth wondered how something that had started out so well could have ended so badly. She wondered what she'd done with her life. She wondered if she'd ever find someone to love her now that she was almost 60 and felt emotionally broken. It took her years to recover enough to date another man.

THIS STORY PROVIDES an extreme example of the potential impacts of phantom romantic love. The point of the story is that phantom romantic love is not a harmless temporary escape into a fairy tale. It can do serious long-term harm.

The capacity to fall in love is neutral rather than good or bad in and of itself. It is a device that can enable you to reach your higher self, either by giving you a glimpse of your true divine nature or the darker side of your soul that cries out for healing. What makes the difference is the stage of development of the lover.

We are most likely to be drawn to a soulmate who is functioning at a similar level of maturity; we'll get into this over the next several pages. Phantom romantic love is most likely to happen at an earlier stage of maturity, when the love experience is likely to blind you to the problems that lie ahead.

Elizabeth and Jason were both young and not fully mature when they met. If Elizabeth had been at a more mature stage of development, it is more likely that she would have found true romantic love with someone. However, stage of development has nothing to do with age. It is all to do with how past-life conditioning interacts with current life conditioning. It is as possible for a 70-year-old to be stuck at an earlier stage of psycho-social development as for a 16-year-old to behave wisely and compassionately beyond their years.

But, just as it is possible for a more mature person to fall in love with a less mature soulmate who continually prevents growth, as was the case for Elizabeth, it's also possible for a more mature soulmate to pull the less-advanced partner forward to their level. When this happens, it's likely a reunion of souls for a karmic reason.

Stages of Development

If true romantic love is so great, why does anyone fall into relationship-employment love or phantom romantic love? We can only answer this question by understanding the stages of development or awareness. All of us, depending on factors such as what we came into this life to learn and what experiences we have in our early lives, enter into any relationship from one of four stages of development. Psychologists generally agree that all humans pass through different stages of psycho-social development as they move through life. The characteristics of these stages are similar among all people, unless psychological trauma or mental illness give rise to unnatural delays. However, different psychologists define and label these stages very differently. In my first book, *Changing Fate Through Reincarnation*, I discussed the nine stages of Jane Loevinger's ego theory.[2] To Loevinger, a developmental psychologist, "ego" means that the ability to synthesize the concept of "who I am" differs at each developmental stage. For our purposes, I have compressed Loevinger's nine stages into just four: codependent, dependent, independent, and interdependent. Understanding key personality traits at each of these stages can help us understand the different needs and desires that motivate a person to fall in love, and recognize that these needs and desires will typically produce very different romantic experiences.

It also helps to understand the role of power in relationships. Several moral-development theorists believe there's a correlation between developmental maturity and where individuals locate moral authority. That is, do they believe the power in their lives is external or internal? This idea is supported by such luminaries as Jean Piaget and Lawrence Kohlberg, who believe the moral authority of people at early stages of moral development is external, dictated by religion, a spiritual teacher, or family.[3] On the other hand, the moral authority of people at mature stages of moral development is both internal and divine. Let's see how this plays out in the personalities at each of these four stages of maturity.

1. CODEPENDENT

At the codependent stage of development, relationships are exploitative and transactional in nature. Partners do not have a strong sense of individual identity. Their sense of self is unclear. Psychologically, they are not mature enough to have a clear psychological separation between "not-I" and "I" because their moral sense of self is still at a symbiotic stage of awareness.

Relationship symbiosis means that each person in a relationship feels they are incomplete without the other, but not in a healthy or loving way.[4] Theoretically, all humans have three ego states: a parent ego, an adult ego and a child ego. A healthy relationship allows both people the flexibility to relate to the other from any one of these ego states. But in a codependent or symbiotic relationship, each partner is only able to use one or two of their ego states and depends on the other to express the remaining state(s). Essentially, they are only one person, and because they are so codependent, they lack the flexibility to step out of unhealthy relationship patterns.

For example, due to events in her childhood, Sandy has a great fear of abandonment. As a result, she feels so small and fearful that she gives in to her husband Eric's humiliating demands.

Like Sandy, Eric feels inadequate, but for a variety of personal and cultural reasons, he expresses these feelings differently. To Eric, Sandy's distorted attachment need provides an opportunity for him to overpower her, which makes him feel the way he believes a "real" man should feel. Both partners need this codependent relationship to justify their existence and perpetuate their self-concept.

But while codependent relationships can be overtly abusive, they can also appear to be very caring. For example, Keith and Wendy have been married for 30 years. Early in their relationship, the power dynamics between them seemed to see-saw back and forth; sometimes Keith would dominate, other times Wendy would, but it always seemed relatively balanced to others. Over the years, however, Keith has had several health crises and has become increasingly physically dependent on Wendy. As this has happened, Wendy has increasingly assumed a "mothering" role, taking care of her husband, while Keith has become increasingly withdrawn from life. Wendy has all the parent and adult ego, while Keith has only the child ego. It's almost as if between the two of them, they make up one person. They tell themselves they are settled, but the truth is they've just settled into a comfortable rut and they're both afraid to ask for more out of the relationship.

2. DEPENDENT

At the dependent stage, people identify who they are in terms of their relationships with others. Unlike people at the codependent stage, they are willing to exchange equitably in the relationship. They play by the rules set by authorities, not because they agree with them but because they are afraid of being punished and being alone.

Despite coming from a loving, supportive home, Ben has always had a strong sense of shame and he gives up easily when facing adversity. He does not accomplish much in his career and he envies rich and famous people while despising unsuccessful people. He is kind, conscientious and giving unless he feels betrayed or crossed, when he can become quite vindictive. He is highly inflexible in the areas of his life over which he feels out of control, and always needs to have the final say. By conventional standards, Ben is a good husband who does not cheat and takes good care of his wife and their children.

Ben's wife, Betty, is his only close friend. Because she does not question him or push him to change, he values her devotion. However, it is an unwritten rule that Betty cannot have a career. The problem is that she *wants* a career, not only for its worldly rewards, but also because she feels personally stagnant. She feels a career could help her to be a better person, but she tells herself that she cannot have everything in life and she is lucky to have such a caring husband.

Weighed down by this self-denial, Betty develops chronic migraines. She loudly asserts her opinions in every situation to unconsciously compensate for her sense of smallness in her marriage. She becomes strongly anti-feminist and trashes women who focus on personal development. Yet, she encourages her daughter to go as far as she can in her career to compensate for what she misses in her own life.

Later in Ben's life, he turns to religion. His innate shame fits well with the religion he follows. He believes his personal salvation must come from a higher power, not himself. Naturally, Betty follows her husband and becomes a fervent believer, which also supports her life choices. Although neither Betty nor Ben is particularly happy, they believe they have a good relationship because they know their respective roles in their marriage. They are matched at a dependent stage of development.

3. INDEPENDENT

People at the independent stage of development are more self-aware. They set their own rules. They are aware of being exceptions to the norm. They have a clear sense of who they are and what they do and don't want, and they're willing to pay the price for what they want. This does not mean they don't need others; it means they have deconstructed their lives and reconstructed their fragmented selves into a balanced, integrated self. They think independently, without relying on external authorities or relationships to define who they are, and they construct their identity based on their own values and beliefs.

Heather and Mike have been together since high school, and each considers the other their best friend. When they first started dating, they did everything together—both were avid snowboarders and loved partying the weekend away with their friends. People said they were "joined at the hip." They were even both planning to pursue careers in marketing, and dreamed of one day starting up an agency together.

Their interests began to diverge in college, when Heather took up the guitar and joined a band. As she spent increasingly more time in clubs and bars, Mike threw himself into his studies, preferring to stay home and read on the weekend. By the time they married in their late twenties, their social and professional lives had very little overlap. Heather had changed her major and gone into social work. She continued to live a "weekend warrior" lifestyle, often taking to the road with her bandmates for out-of-town gigs, while Mike became more and more of a homebody all the time.

To the surprise of everyone around them, this shift in direction did not break them apart. Far from feeling threatened or shut out of each other's very different activities, they actively encourage each other to go and do their own thing. In fact, Heather and Mike have a remarkably low-conflict marriage. Of course, like all couples, they annoy and disappoint each other from time to time. But because their live-and-let-live approach to hobbies also extends to their communication style, they almost never challenge each other on their problematic behaviour. Instead of facing up to their own or each other's difficult emotions, they deal with hurt feelings by becoming even more wrapped up in their personal interests. Mike and Heather love and respect each other a great deal, but they are more like roommates, or perhaps brother and sister, than life partners walking a shared path.

4. INTERDEPENDENT

At the interdependent stage, individuals have an integrated wholeness created by synthesizing the conflicts they face in life. They appreciate each individual's uniqueness and value the interdependence among people. They intensely appreciate other people's viewpoints. Their sense of self incorporates virtuous qualities that include others in their personal identity, and consequently they radiate a sense of maturity and universality.

When Eileen, a British medical doctor, decides to volunteer her services to a refugee camp in Somalia, things start out well enough. But soon, her strong personality is clashing with that of the Algerian-born administrator, Ali. Although Eileen second-guesses her decision to work here, she never backs down. However, instead of being confrontational with Ali, she decides to find out why he does not allow her to provide medical care in the way she thinks is best for the refugees in the camp. In getting to know Ali, she realizes he has a compassionate heart and open attitude. She finds a lot of commonalities between them; the main difference is that, owing to customs and traditions Eileen is not familiar with, Ali expresses his caring in a different way. In allowing herself to learn from him, she falls in love with him. For Ali's part, he appreciates Eileen's strong will, compassionate heart and beautiful soul, and falls in love with her.

In their ongoing struggles with each other, Eileen helps Ali realize that his love for the refugees is masked by the fear of abandonment he experienced in his childhood. At the same time, Eileen realizes that her true motive in coming to Africa was not to escape the red tape of the UK's medical system but to find a life that is worth living. As a medical doctor in the UK, she had all the worldly things a middle-class woman could want, yet her life felt empty. She wanted to cry all the time but had no tears. Since working in the refugee camp, she's remembered why she studied medicine in the first place. The pain of the refugees has awakened her soul. Even though her material life is far from comfortable, this is where her heart belongs. Because Eileen and Ali reveal their vulnerable selves in each other's presence, they forge a deep bond.

Later, Ali and Eileen discover corruption on the part of the camp's private sponsor and they work together to try to save the camp. Fighting for a shared cause takes their intimacy to another level. In the other person, they each find strength they lack, and they respect each other's uniqueness. Their interdependent relationship is grounded in love through which they continue to flourish individually and as a couple.

Which Stages Lead to Which Kinds of Love?

Clearly, it's going to be very difficult—not impossible, perhaps, but difficult—for people operating at the codependent and dependent stages to enter into a true romantic love relationship. At these stages, people are very focused on satisfying their own needs, which may have gone unmet when they were children. Therefore, at these stages, we are far more likely to fall into relationship-employment love. We have a list of needs and we look for someone who can meet them. If that person meets our needs well, we could be happy enough in the relationship to believe that this is love, like Betty and Ben. Or we might recognize we're not in love, but decide that we are comfortable enough, like Keith and Wendy. On the other hand, we may be compelled to seek out partners who reinforce our most negative feelings about ourselves, and that inevitably leads to unhealthy and unhappy relationships, as with Sandy and Eric.

It is sometimes possible for people to evolve out of one relationship stage into another if both partners are willing to work at it. Mike and Heather have developed an avoidance-based coping mechanism that neither one has the relationship skills or inclination to change. Their habit of never rocking the boat has kept them together over the years while their friends have fallen in and out of many messy relationships. But if one or both of them were prepared to go out on a limb and reveal their fears and burdens to the other, their strong couple bond just might see them through the initial discomfort and bring their relationship a new dimension of closeness, intimacy and personal discovery.

Many people don't like the concept of developmental stages at all because they fear it must mean they are inadequate if they are at an earlier developmental stage. But there is no more reason to judge a person's stage of psychological development than to judge a child's stage of chronological development. All of us go through this developmental sequence, or something like it. So it's not good or bad; it's just the way nature, psychology, and spirituality are.

All of us except a few spiritual founders are on the same sacred path of spiritual growth. Every one of us is at a particular developmental stage. Our true nature is love. We are here to transform our human qualities so that the divine love in us can shine through. We all go through this awakening journey. When we advance our stage of development, it does not mean we are morally superior to people who are at a less mature stage of development. It just means we are more aware that our true nature is love, and better prepared to align our ego-self with that truth.

Another important reason we all have to go through this developmental journey is that our spiritual development is not only about ourselves. Because our true nature, love, is interdependent, it is our spiritual responsibility to help others awaken. When we grow, we want to help others who are stuck in their unconsciousness. But how can we do that if we are ignorant about their experiences, pains and needs? Because we have first-person experience on this sacred path, we know how to help. We know and understand how painful it is to feel emptiness and loneliness in relationship employment or to feel something is still missing in relationship-employment love. This is why everyone has to walk through this developmental journey stage by stage in order to become a teacher—a life teacher who will use our love to awaken the love that is already in the soulmates we meet over the course of our life journey.

Phantom romantic love can also, in itself, spur spiritual growth. For the last several years that Elizabeth was in the phantom romantic-love relationship, her life seemed like it was on a slow boat to hell. And immediately after she emerged from it, she thought she'd arrived in hell. But in time, she turned her attention to learning the life and moral lessons the phantom relationship had to offer, thus transforming the toxic pain she'd been experiencing for years into growing pain that allowed her to continue maturing. (More on that in Chapter 6.)

On a final note, there can be other reasons besides relationship employment or phantom love why a soulmate may not inspire you to grow and change, and we've already touched on some of them. One reason is timing—you're simply not ready to grow at the time you reconnect. Another reason could be that the most important lesson you need to learn in this life is not with this particular soulmate. In each lifetime, we cross paths with numerous soulmates who can, if we're open, teach us different lessons. In Chapter 1, Anna's most important life lesson is with her secret lover. Her husband is also a soulmate, but in the script of this life he is merely in the supporting cast. That doesn't mean his role is insignificant. In fact, without him, there would be no conflict in the Anna's heart, and that conflict is the source of the lesson she is here to learn.

The depth of the spiritual lessons you learn with a soulmate may not have any direct correlation with the duration of your time together. You might spend 40 years with a partner and learn virtually nothing. Or you might have one transformational month with a soulmate who changes the course of your destiny, never to see them again.

FURTHER CONSIDERATION

- Have you ever used a compatibility checklist to screen romantic partners? If so, what do you expect from your life partner? If you used it in the past and formed a long-term relationship on that basis, how did it work out? If you had to do it over again, how would you change that list, or would you use it at all?

- Why do you take relationship workshops or read books like this one? What do you hope to get out of them? How does that usually work out for you?

- What qualities in yourself would you consider most likely to bring out the qualities you're seeking in a partner? What qualities are you lacking that you would like to develop to attract the kind of partner you're seeking?

- Does the concept of relationship employment fit any relationships you've experienced? Has it evolved into relationship-employment love? If you've never been in relationship-employment love, do you know a couple who have? How has it seemed to work out, either for you or for a couple you know?

- What are the key differences between true romantic love and phantom romantic love? What are the differences between the people who fall in true romantic love and those who fall in phantom romantic love? Describe a time in your life when you may have fallen in phantom romantic love.

- Define the concept of the shadow self. Which of your own personality traits would you describe as characterizing your shadow self?

- How does your relationship help you to be the best you can be, and to see yourself, your partner and life at a deeper level? How does it help your partner with that? Describe any obstacles that may be preventing this from happening.

- How do you feel about the concept of stages of development? Do you find it helpful or not? What stage do you think you're at and why? What stage do you think your partner is at and why? What stage do you think your relationship is at and why? Are you happy with this stage? If not, how would you like it to change and how do you think you might go about that?

FIVE

Passion and Sex

SPIRITUALITY AND SEX have long been uneasy bedfellows. Many religions and spiritual traditions advocate celibacy or chastity to their followers. This, it is felt, encourages them to be mindful of their connection with the divine, and to devote their intention, attention and concentration to deepening that connection. Although different religions have their own perspectives on sex, a common doctrine is the sublimation of physical pleasure. The thinking is that the devout will not be distracted by sensory desires. Some orders take vows of poverty for the same reason. But the writings of some mystics also suggest that celibacy allows religious practitioners to redirect their sexual energies to experiencing unity with God as if in a state of sexual fusion. Some Western mystics even liken their spiritual experiences to having sex with God. Consider the following poem by St. John of the Cross.

THE DARK NIGHT

One dark night,
fired with love's urgent longings
—ah, the sheer grace!—
I went out unseen,
my house being now all stilled.

In darkness, and secure,
by the secret ladder, disguised,
—ah, the sheer grace!—
in darkness and concealment,
my house being now all stilled.

On that glad night,
in secret, for no one saw me,
nor did I look at anything,
with no other light or guide
than the One that burned in my heart.

This guided me
more surely than the light of noon
to where he was awaiting me
—him I knew so well—
there in a place where no one appeared.

O guiding night!
O night more lovely than the dawn!
O night that has united
the Lover with his beloved,
transforming the Beloved into his Lover.

Upon my flowering breast,
which I kept wholly for him alone,

there he lay sleeping,
and I caressing him
there in a breeze from the fanning cedars.

When the breeze blew from the turret,
as I parted his hair,
wounded my neck
with its gentle hand,
suspending all my senses.

I abandoned and forgot myself,
laying my face on my Beloved;
all things ceased; I went out from myself,
leaving my cares
forgotten among the lilies. [1]

This Christian mystic is clearly on fire, having sex with God—or something very close to it! This spiritual, sexual and mystical experience is not exclusive to Christianity. My favourite poet, the thirteenth-century Sufi philosopher Rumi, wrote many poems describing this sexual, ecstatic and mystical state of consciousness.

If you are not planning to become a nun or monk who mates with God, what would the potentially mystical aspects of sex have to do with your love life? Well, just as celibates can use their sexual energy to connect with the divine, true romantic lovers can use their sexual energy with their beloved to do the same. In fact, many of the world's faiths have esoteric erotic traditions that practitioners use in this way. For example, tantric sexual practice has played an important role in cultivating union with the divine for two thousand years. Certain Taoist sects use sexual energy to help practitioners become immortals and gods.[2] And some Tibetan Buddhist sects use sexual union as a path to enlightenment.[3]

In other words, you don't need to retreat to a monastery to train your body, mind and soul to achieve ecstatic union. Cultivating a sense of oneness in the midst of sex with your lover can help you nurture other ways to merge your realities. When you're in true romantic love, the oneness that comes from the breakdown of "I" and "Not-I" can express itself in many ways, such as sex, a leisurely walk together on a warm fall afternoon, or a winter evening spent basking in the glow of a cozy fire.

It is natural that, when two people fall in love, they crave sexual union in much the same way religious celibates crave union with their beloved and channel their sexual energies into achieving it. But that doesn't mean sex is the only way for two lovers to glimpse the divine. And it doesn't mean sex will always or ever connect two lovers with the divine. Like meditation, the relational path can only be part of a spiritual path when it's practised with intention, attention and concentration. Without these key components, sex is just sex. Or it's just copulating.

Copulating, Having Sex or Making Love

Humans are one of only a few species that engage in sexual intercourse for recreation as well as procreation. Most people recognize that sex can have an emotional function, as a way to express love, and I am clearly not alone in believing it also has a spiritual function, to connect with the divine. How well sex expresses what's in our souls depends on the quality of our minds. In Chinese philosophy, the mind also means the heart, which includes the spirit (soul). The Chinese call this "shen." The mind and heart are two sides of the same coin; our feelings and thoughts together determine whether we are copulating, having sex or making love. I would argue that only in a relationship based on true romantic love are we actually making love, a qualitative evaluation that's contingent upon two lovers bringing intention, attention and concentration to the act of sexual intercourse.

As I define them, the concepts of copulating, having sex and making love imply certain intentions, desires, experiences and attitudes. It is possible for a person to copulate with one individual, have sex with another and make love with a third. The sexual act is the same; the difference is in the intention, attention and concentration, which can transform sex from a purely biological function into a meditative practice that unifies the biological, psychological and spiritual realms.

The difference is in the quality of love and the energy that the lovers bring to the sexual act. Most people are aware that there is a relationship between the mind and the body, but they have no awareness of the relationship between the mind and energy. Energy appears to be an abstract and exotic concept, yet it is possible to feel the bio-energy in your body, which has magnetic and vibrating qualities.

Try an experiment. Open your hand so it's facing upward. Ask your partner to open their hand but facing downward with about half an inch between your two palms. Focus your attention on the center of your and your partner's palms. After a while, when your mind is very quiet, you should feel a bio-electrical magnetic field between your palm and theirs. The Chinese believe intention leads energy (chi) and energy moves blood. Western biofeedback techniques confirm this. If you focus your attention on your palm, blood will flow to your hand and the temperature of that hand will rise. The point is that the mind has a role in directing energy flow in the body. It is not mystical; we can train our minds to do this at will.

Now let's look at how intention, attention and concentration work in sex.

Copulation

In a classic case of copulation, you don't need to like your sexual partner or even know them. They are merely a sexual object. Your intention, attention and concentration are on using your partner to release sexual tension in your body. You're giving pleasure to yourself, essentially masturbating with a partner. Your attention and intention are on your genitals or in your head, and consequently that's where your energy goes.

When two people copulate, they're likely to need sexual fantasies to achieve orgasm. Since your mind determines the sensory and energetic range of your vibrational field, and since your mind is focused on your fantasy, you will not feel a deep connection with your partner. Moreover, since your fantasy takes you out of the present moment, you may even have a hard time achieving orgasm.

There's nothing wrong with this. Sometimes people who are not in a relationship need sexual release. As long as both partners know what they're doing is copulating and the act is between mutually consenting adults, I say, have at it!

It's also possible to copulate in a relationship. For example, if two people are in a long-term codependent or dependent relationship, there may be very little emotion left in their sexual interactions. Sex may be an act of mutual masturbation. And they may be okay with that. Who is anyone else to judge?

To me, the point in discussing the quality of coitus is to show how it can, when practised with intention, attention and concentration, express true romantic love. But so can all of our daily actions. In my mind, the qualitative differences in sex have no moral implications. What motivates two consenting adults to have intercourse is their business.

Having Sex

To have sex with a partner involves caring and affection, and possibly even feelings of love. This is not meaningless or anonymous and it's not mutual masturbation. Your mental image of your sexual partner is of a person you care for. When you are kissing and caressing them, it's more than kissing just any warm body. You're not having sex as a vehicle for reproduction or sexual release but because it helps you feel closer to each other.

When we are in a relationship that on some level is still working, we have a special image/thought-form of our sexual partner. In this regard, we are having sex with an image/thought-form in our mind. We use sex to breathe energy into this image/thought-form.

Again, there's nothing wrong with this as long as both partners know this is what they're doing. You can have sex with someone you're not in love with. That's essentially the definition of "friends with benefits." You care about the person, but you're not in love with them. They're a stand-in for someone you might love someday. You might also have sex in the earlier stages of a codependent or dependent relationship. As you're likely in relationship-employment love, it's unlikely the sex will be a spiritual experience, but it can go beyond releasing sexual tension or trying to reproduce and become a deeply satisfying expression of mutual affection.

Making Love

True romantic lovemaking transforms subject "I" and object "you" into transcendental unity. In this special state, the boundary between subject and object breaks down and the two merge into one. This could mean either that two distinct vibrational systems are merging into a bigger whole, or that they are in tune with each other's frequencies and creating a harmonic effect.

A couple who have had the experience of true romantic lovemaking know that it far exceeds having sex. Apart from safety and trust, it requires that two souls are in love with each other. The experience of intimacy surpasses the psychological closeness of a couple having sex. Even the most skilful lover cannot offer this to a sexual partner without sincere intention.

When a person is in love, their five senses open and their

awareness expands. In this state, the lovers' bodies and minds unite and sexual energy flows freely. The lovers are aware of their physical, emotional and energetic states. This awareness is a pre-requisite for psychic awareness. Mindfulness meditation trains the meditator to be more self-aware, but when we fall in love, we need no training. A lover's body/mind union empowers them to build a temporary psychic connection with the beloved. The two lovers can easily achieve a state of energetic union because the vibrational frequency (the deeper inner state) of their bodies, minds and spirits are in tune with each other.

One way to define the word intercourse is "communication." It is a means of connecting two persons. To communicate at an energetic level, both partners must surrender to each other. In the course of making love, an act of pure intention is an act of unconditional giving. The lovers are naturally mindful to their beloved's bodily, emotional and energetic state. In a moment like this, of deep communion, nothing exists for each of them but their beloved.

Making love creates unity. Making love creates the energetic body of the relationship and the new identities the two lovers assume as a result. The intensity of this energetic body strengthens the relationship and transforms having sex into making love.

Sexual Passion

In her 1993 book *Are You the One for Me?* American relation-ship guru Barbara De Angelis argues that porn destroys intimacy. "If you're making love with your partner and fantasizing about having sex with someone else, you are cheating on your partner," she writes. "You're breaking [faith] by deliberately focusing your sexual attention on someone else."[4] She clearly calls consuming pornography a form of infidelity. I wholeheartedly agree with this, yet this phenomenon is widespread and appears natural. Why?

One reason is that there is no love in the relationship at all. We are attracted to our marital partner initially because we are looking for a relationship employee or employer. Two elements, passion and attachment, make relationship-employment love different than romantic love, giving romantic love an enchanting dimension that no other form of love equates to. Generally speaking, if a couple enjoys passion and attachment in their relationship, they should have no need for pornography or fantasy.

Sex plays an important role in many couples' relationships, especially in the initial stages of a relationship. Many of us are attracted to our beloved because of the sexual dimension of romantic love. The problem is that once the sexual passion subsides, many couples fall out of love. Why can so few couples maintain their sexual passion throughout their relationship?

Many scientists and psychologists believe sexual energy is a biological drive whereas love is a psychological need, and therefore sex and love bear no relationship to each other. This leads to the problem with many popular relationship self-help books penned by scientists and psychologists, which is that spirituality has no place in their worldview. Even when some enlightened psychologists and therapists try to bring spirituality into their theories of love, they lack adequate conceptual tools to explain the connection.

If we return to Eastern wisdom, we can find some insights into the spiritual dimension of romantic love, sex and relationships. For example, in Chinese Taoism, chi means life force. From the perspective of Chinese Medicine, chi is intimately tied to the functional aspects of the five major internal organs, which are physical, and each organ correlates to a specific emotion, which is psychological. In other words, there is a relationship between sexual energy and physical and psychological health. Passion—intense emotional energy—intimately links to sexual energy. The source of passion is the yearning of our souls, embodied in images/thought-forms. Very often, our conscious minds are unaware of this particular image/thought-form. The presence of our beloved brings out the yearning in our unconsciousness.

When we link all the above concepts together, we see that the passion fuelled by sexual energy energizes the human soul.

Sexual energy is transformed into spiritual energy when a lover thinks of their beloved. To keep this image/thought-form alive, its creator must continue to supply it with life force in the form of sexual energy. (For our purposes, sexual energy and life force are synonymous.) If the lover's soul does not bring forth a special image/thought-form or if they do not continually breathe life force into that image/thought-form, the image/thought-form will fade. Pure sexual energy is biological, and can therefore be worn down. And, if sexual energy is driven by personality, it becomes emotional; it may take longer to expire, but it's difficult for most of us to maintain a deeply emotional connection over many years, so this, too, can be worn down. But when sexual energy is driven by the soul, it becomes spiritual, and spiritual energy can last, I believe, indefinitely.

Because of the multi-dimensionality of human nature, sexual union can have different effects. If it is pure physical play, the excitation of sexual energy between two lovers can have positive biological pleasure, but the connection, if any, stays in the physical realm. If the couple experiences closeness and an early stage of intimacy, sexual pleasure has an additional dimension of socio-psychological pleasure. If it becomes a conduit for the union of two souls, the two lovers may experience spiritual fusion. This may be why both Indian and Chinese spiritual traditions independently discovered ways to transform sexual energy to aid spiritual development.

Monogamy and Philosophy

I describe myself as a spiritual existentialist. Existentialism—to me—is a philosophy based on the belief that we come into this world alone, we live alone and we die alone, each of us separated from others by our autonomous subjective reality. This sense of aloneness makes us want to connect with others. The problem is that we can only connect with others meaningfully when we know ourselves.

Unfortunately, in our culture, most of us are afraid to connect too well with ourselves, because getting to know ourselves intimately can be a painful experience. Consequently, we disconnect from ourselves, which makes it difficult, if not impossible, for us to share our subjective reality with anyone. Even though we may interact with people every day, we find ourselves talking without speaking and hearing without listening, like the people in Simon and Garfunkel's famous song "Sound of Silence," in which no one dares disturb the sound of silence. What Paul Simon is saying is that people are afraid to share. Sharing could risk pain. People don't want to risk pain, so they stay in their own little worlds. What follows is alienation and isolation, but, ironically, the loneliness and emptiness that arise when people cannot find anyone, including a partner with whom to share their subjective reality, are also very painful.

I describe myself as a spiritual existentialist because I believe, on a physical plane, we come into the world alone, live alone and die alone, but if we get in touch with our spirituality, we can join with others on a much deeper level and find the unity that eludes us when we think of life as a purely materialistic phenomenon. Spirituality brings joy and hope to a philosophy I find honest and realistic but that, without spirituality, would be almost unbearably bleak.

With this understanding of what underpins my approach to life, I'd like to share a story about an experience I had some time ago when I attended a philosophical meetup where the discussion topic was Jean-Paul Sartre's existentialism. I'd had prior conversations with the group leader. Sartre was his idol, and he'd shared with me how this twentieth-century French philosopher's brand of existentialism had influenced his own way of being. I was particularly delighted to hear that the discussion for that meetup would focus on love, marriage and sex from an existential perspective, which I had been researching for more than twenty years.

After opening the meeting with an introduction of Sartre's philosophy, the group leader asked, "What is the intention of the institution of marriage? Given our way of life in the twenty-first century, if marriage cannot satisfy our need for passion and love, should we stick with one woman for life or should we, like Sartre, have an open relationship?" The group quickly agreed that, since men were not made to be monogamous and the purpose of marriage was purely to satisfy basic domestic needs, we should have other lovers. Love is about sex, they all said, and therefore Sartre's open relationship with his lover, Simone de Beauvoir, made a good relationship model to solve men's existential needs.

I guess I forgot to take my emotional intelligence to that meeting, because after listening somewhat incredulously to this near-unanimous opinion for several minutes, I blurted out angrily, "What about sacrifice, sharing and pain, which are essential to true love? If a man is not willing to give up sexual freedom for his beloved, what kind of love is that? Is love really the same as sex? If sex is all love is, why use the word 'love' at all? Who are you trying to convince, someone else or yourselves? What about your woman's needs? Why bother to marry a woman in the first place?"

The more I talked, the angrier I felt. "No wonder Sartre was an atheist existentialist. When de Beauvoir screamed at him about the unhappiness and emptiness she felt in their relationship, he must have been thinking, 'Thank God this is the only life I have.'" I left it at that. The rest of the group glanced at each other and shifted in their seats. After a few moments of silence, the conversation continued. I was not surprised that the group leader never invited me to another existentialism meetup.

What do you think about Sartre's brand of existentialism? Did this philosopher truly grasp the essence of existence, life and love or did he manufacture his philosophy to justify his life experience and personal, selfish desires? Love, sex and relationships are existential concerns. Our choices and actions are reflections of who we are and what we want to make of our lives. I don't believe the existential philosophy through which I attempt to understand life is empty talk, but a way of being, a way of relating, connecting and living. A lifelong friendship between Sartre and de Beauvoir kept them stuck in a "romantic" relationship with each other, but the relationship itself, and the pain it generated, was toxic. (We'll talk more about toxic pain in Chapter 6.)

If you want a flourishing love rather than a relationship like the one Sartre and de Beauvoir shared, you may want to reflect deeply on the messages about passion and sex in this chapter. Because although it is not difficult to join our naked bodies together, it is not always so easy for us to open our hearts. This is because the heart exists in two dimensions, the physical and the energetic. We may not want or know how to open our hearts, which makes sharing one's subjective experience with another person, even a spouse, a daunting challenge.

This could be so if, as individuals, we have no sense of unity between body and mind, conscious and unconscious, emotional and spiritual, in the first place. Without such unity, we can have no emotional connection with a partner. Because emotional connection is preceded by emotional attunement, which is the most fundamental element of moral capacity in humanity, we cannot experience a sense of unity at a higher level.

One of the most profound distances between you and your partner is when your bodies are joined together, but you know you are not in love with this person. You lie to yourself and to your partner by feigning feelings for them. You care about your spouse because it is your responsibility and duty. However, this moral feeling is not romantic love and it can't fill the void in your heart.

Another challenging distance between you and your partner opens up when you don't feel safe around them physically or emotionally. You do not trust them. You want to get as far away as possible from them but you have nowhere to go.

Sometimes emotional and psychological distance can arise spontaneously. Initially, you may feel close to your beloved because you think you know them. But one day, you feel a huge distance between the two of you and realize you don't really know them at all. You realize you've misunderstood yourself, and therefore you've misunderstood your beloved.

If you don't know yourself, how can you know your partner? Of course, if you spend five to ten years of your life with someone, you know their habits, attitudes and preferences inside out. You can predict their behaviour. In fact, the more unconscious your partner is, the easier it is for you to predict their habitual patterns of reaction. But this kind of bonding is not much different than bonding with your dog. Although you learn your dog's habits within four to six months, you can't define this bond as intimacy because a prerequisite of intimacy is the fusion of two minds, each with reflective consciousness.

Knowing your partners' habitual thoughts, feelings and behaviour patterns does not mean you know your partner. There are many stories about people finding out that their late partners, or their ex-partners, were never in love with them. In this case, the couple spends their entire adult life together, sleeping in the same bed, raising children, touching each other's bodies, yet not knowing each other well enough to make a deep connection with their hearts, minds and souls.

Perhaps the distance between you and your partner arises because you are merely playing a persona in life. You know who you are in the relationship is not the real you; you are simply playing a role in the relationship. A typical example is marrying your spouse for economic, social or reproductive reasons. Your heart is still in the past, perhaps with the first lover you had in your teens. You are playing the role of dutiful wife or husband in the current relationship.

Another gap between you and the person you love is being unable to communicate how you truly feel to this particular person. You have difficulty saying, "I love you" for whatever reason. Or you cannot honestly tell your partner that although you admire them, you don't feel sexually excited by them anymore.

Life Passion

People often equate passion and sex. But passion is more than that. Regardless of whether we are experiencing relationship-employment love or true romantic love, over time we tend to lose sexual passion for our beloved. This is because the sudden excitable pleasure that newness brings does not last forever, as the human brain is wired to desensitize to repeated stimuli. It is in our nature that once the novelty of a new partner has worn off, our desire for them becomes less urgent.

Another reason we lose sexual passion is that we confuse falling in lust with falling in love. If we view another human being primarily as a sexual object there will be a sexual urge but no passion. When that urge inevitably fades, nothing remains in its place.

Deeper than a sexual urge, sexual passion is a vital force in romantic love; it's why we are physically attracted to our partners and we want to do something with those desires. Indeed, the passion we feel when we fall in love always has a sexual component. But what is passion?

In this book, the concepts of inspiration and passion can be considered cousins. Passion is intense emotional energy that enables us to express our inspiration outwardly. We breathe life force (passion) into the image/thought-form brought forth to our consciousness. Thus, passion, like inspiration, has two components: life force (sexual energy) and image/thought-form. Passion is an emotion that gives rise to fervent enthusiasm about an object, which can be a person, an action or a thing.

The difference between excitement and enthusiasm is that excitement is a short-lived state of arousal caused by a need met or the anticipation of a need being met. The current meaning of enthusiasm is strong excitement or active interest, but the older meaning had connotations of religious inspiration. Since passion is an emotion, it also has a component of attitude. When a lover falls in true romantic love, their arousal is more than physical excitement; it's enthusiasm and even awe from the calling of the soul. When the soul comes alive, the lover uses passion to express themselves. I call this *life passion*.

Falling in love is like the eruption of a volcano. It can consume everything around it. The power of the explosion has an inverse relationship with time. The shorter the time required to release the energy, the more power and intensity is generated. Yet passion can endure if it is life passion brought forth by our souls. Because life passion is about who we are and the kind of life we want to live to express that—once this life passion is found, it will stay with us till the day our bodies die.

Life passion is not any activity that merely arouses or excites our interest and curiosity temporarily. It can last an entire lifetime if it aligns with our true nature because it is a calling from our soul. This means that when we know we've found something or someone to live for, some purpose or person worth our effort and sacrifice, we continuously breathe life force (passion) into them, and that makes us who we are.

At the end of his 1974 classic *Zen and the Art of Motorcycle Maintenance*, author Robert M. Pirsig talks about his journey in publishing the book.[5] The publisher's expectations of the book's prospects were so low that he told Pirsig not to expect any additional royalties. The only reason he, the publisher, purchased it in the first place was as a reminder of why he had become an editor and publisher—he loved knowledge and he wanted to publish books that were worthy even if they weren't profitable. The man was an idealist. (This is the kind of publisher I admire.) *Zen and the Art of Motorcycle Maintenance* became a modern classic that has sold more than five million copies.

The publisher of *Zen* found an outlet to express his life passion, and this passion stayed with him for his whole career. But if we don't keep nurturing our passion, it can go dormant. When this happens, we lose our self-awareness and our gut instinct diminishes. When that happens, we need the vibrational energy of something to wake up our soul and remind us of our life passion. In this way, life passion can last.

Many people experience the intensity of falling in love. Most are concerned with keeping the passion alive so their love will not fade away, even if they have no interest in growing into a better human being. Transforming sexual passion into life passion requires the lover to have reached a certain stage of maturity.

So how do you transform the explosive sexual passion at the time of falling in love to the enduring life passion of being in love? Experiencing true romantic love and keeping passion alive throughout your relationship requires spiritual growth, whether you want it or not. The source of true romantic love and life passion is the soul. The feeling we experience when falling in love is *more* than a feeling. We find the person who matters to us and makes us want to live. They make us look forward to the next day. This aliveness consumes our whole being—we live in it, we breathe it in and we're even willing to die for it. It is the seed of life passion, and as Pirsig's story shows, life passion does not die.

If we live with life passion, our energy becomes the source of self-motivation. We direct our energy to the person and things we are passionate about. Instead of being forced by social responsibility to do things we don't want to do, we do them voluntarily and happily. Depending on our level of maturity, our passion for life may turn into universal love, like that of Mohandas Gandhi or Nelson Mandela. These sages lived their lives passionately. Their passions ignited energy in millions of people from around the world, inspiring them to live their lives with a higher purpose.

Friendship

If you experience true romantic love and your partner breathes life force into you, motivating you to grow and pursue your life passion, will your passion end with your partner's physical death or separation?

Simply, no. Let's say that, because you've found a partner who truly believes in you, you have decided to confront and solve something in your life that has troubled you—perhaps drug or alcohol addiction. In the course of your recovery, you find a new sense of purpose and life passion when you decide to become an addictions counsellor. Tragically, your partner is killed in a car accident. Yet the spirit of their love and belief in you lives on in your soul. Your romantic awakening has become embedded within you. Your initial sexual passion transformed into deep friendship with your beloved, which in turn became a life passion that in turn fuelled the romantic and sexual relationship. Even with their death, and in the face of unspeakable grief, your soul has been transformed. Your earthly separation from them (though you may reunite in another life) cannot undo that transformation.

Aristotle, one of the most important thinkers in human history, separated friendship into three levels. At the first level, two people exploit each other for their own needs. At the second level, both friends enjoy each other's company and the pleasure they create in the relationship. At the third, both friends enjoy each other's goodness and help each other be the best each can be.[6] This insight illustrates developmental-stage implications for friendships. I would add a fourth level, at which two friends are willing to suffer with each other.

When a couple is codependent, there is no friendship between them. They are in the relationship to exploit each other and satisfy their own needs. If they are at a dependent stage of development, they spend time as friends and lovers because they each get something out of the experience. Yet when a couple moves up to the independent and interdependent stages of development, not only will they want to enjoy the pleasure of life with their lovers and friends, they will want to be the best they can be in this life. They will also hope for the same for their lovers and friends, and the friendship between them will bring out their compassion and help them accomplish that goal.

People at the dependent stage so deeply need safety and security that they refuse to take risks to find their true calling in life. They do everything they can to create repetitive patterns in order to feel protected and anchored. This creates security, but it also creates boredom. Sadly, the number-one killer of passion, whether in life or in a relationship, is boredom. With boredom, we lose our enthusiasm for our partners and the love we once had. Eventually, life and our partners become so predictable they do not inspire us at all. They may even make us angry.

As repetition and boredom eat away at passion, our minds disconnect from our souls. We forget why we fell in love, like when Pirsig's editor forgot what motivated him to be in publishing in the first place. We stop encouraging each other to achieve personal excellence. We don't follow through on the calling in life that gives us passion to live and to love. Fearing relationship breakup, we deny our soul's calling and do not allow ourselves to feel, do, or think freely, or to reflect on who we truly are. Our souls grow cold and numb as our life passion crawls into a cave to hibernate.

Although hibernation looks like little more than sleep, it takes a lot of energy. That's why animals that hibernate instinctively fatten themselves up in the summer and fall; they need to store up enough energy to get themselves through a long, cold winter with little to eat. Similarly, repressing one's innermost feelings and vulnerabilities while pretending to be happy in a relationship demands a tremendous amount of energy. How can two people invest energy in a relationship with each other when they're expending most of their life energy on repression and pretense? In true friendship, as in true love, you encourage your friends (lovers) to grow, to be the best they can be. In true friendship, you can be who you truly are without fear of being judged. Two people in true romantic love breathe life into the true friendship they've built.

There is a practical benefit in building an authentic friendship in a marital relationship. As discussed, it is human nature to want to be with people who make us feel good, not by flattery but by authentic appreciation. If we have a choice, we will always choose friends who help us help ourselves. This makes us feel good because we're encouraged to find our true calling—the calling that makes us feel we not only exist but we truly matter. If two lovers' minds continue to grow afresh as they challenge each other to grow, how can their relationship ever become stale?

But growth can be scary. There is always a real possibility that two lovers will grow at different paces, that one will outgrow the other or both will outgrow the relationship. In this case, although the love relationship might end, the friendship could remain—if it's built on mature qualities.

Moreover, just as certainty creates boredom, uncertainty creates alertness. When two lovers strive for growth, they do not know what will happen to each other and to their relationship the next day, but that gives them incentive to work hard at keeping their relationship fresh and alive. Because uncertainty creates risk, the two lovers cherish what they have in the moment and work to preserve it.

Whom would you choose—a partner who makes you feel good in bed and socially, or the one with whom you'd endured suffering through which you'd become a better person? Odds are you would choose the one with whom you had a transformational experience, as this is a sound basis for friendship.

Sacred Sex

Most people have experienced orgasm, but this is nothing but an intense muscular contraction accompanied by the secretion of hormones. Even if two lovers climax simultaneously, it does not mean they have experienced the intimacy of oneness. In a state of energetic union, people may experience "valley" orgasm. Theoretically, this is when all chakras and meridian channels are open and vibrate in sync and in harmony, inducing wave after wave of energetic pulsation throughout the body. When two lovers are in this transcendental state, the sensory boundary dissolves while the continuum of pulsation goes on. If we are truly in the present moment with our sexual partners, there is no room for fantasy.

Since the 1960s, many spiritual teachers have come to the West to teach various esoteric lovemaking techniques. At the same time, many Western researchers have researched sexuality and produced books, videos and workshops that teach sexual techniques. Because many people have a more-is-better attitude and a speed-dating expectation of love, they have no time for dilly-dallying. They want results, and fast. To make sex/love consumers feel the information they've purchased is worth the money, commercialized teachers and/or researchers pack as much information as possible into their programs, including postures, forms, breathing and other lovemaking techniques. Yet, these consumers miss the secret source of esoteric lovemaking—the mind.

I understand why Western researchers miss this vital concept in their teachings, but I also have strong reservations about spiritual teachers who share esoteric lovemaking techniques. Relatively speaking, it is not that difficult to learn physical postures and techniques. On the other hand, if you have practised meditation, you know how difficult it is to still the mind and sense the inner vibration in your own body. Esoteric sexual training demands that practitioners work for many years at meditation and qigong to balance the meridians and chakras before they feel the effects of the physical postures.

If you are not trained in meditation, or qigong, will you be able to experience the ecstasy of oneness? In a word, yes. With love, you don't need to learn any fancy spiritual or sexual techniques to reach the intimacy of oneness. When two lovers have healthy minds and bodies, and if they are truly in love with each other, with no conditions attached to love and sex, their two hearts and minds will be in sync with each other and their five senses will open. When they touch the body of their beloved, they will transmit their love vibration deep into their beloved's body and soul. As long as two lovers bring pure intention and complete mindfulness and concentration, they are, in essence, meditating while making love. How far this fusion goes depends on the extent to which two lovers give in to each other so both can lose themselves in the process. The more two lovers surrender to each other, the more their sensory, emotional and energetic boundaries dissolve, and the stronger unity they experience.

Commercialized lovemaking techniques that are designed to improve the quality of copulation may help to improve sensory experience. But if your intention is to learn how to make love in a way that deepens emotional and spiritual union, no amount of expensive training will help. You will not see results if your heart is not in it, making love with your partner, and vice versa. The only thing you and your partner need to learn is to develop a personality structure—that is, gain emotional maturity—that will enable both of you to create a relationship based on true romantic love.

Sex becomes boring and loses its novelty and excitement when we are not truly in the present moment with our partner. At this point, pornography and sexual fantasies will not bring it back. With love, our intention, attention and concentration are heightened. In this loving, meditative state, the divine consciousness in the background of our awareness unifies with our experiential self to experience oneness with others and the cosmos. Sex cannot become mechanical if we allow love's energy to guide us.

When two lovers attune to each other bodily, emotionally and energetically, they slip into a call-response state of consciousness. Call-response attunement is the ultimate creativity. When two lovers are in free-flowing attunement while making love, they experience the freshness of life in their sexuality. Spiritually induced sexual ecstasy far exceeds sexual pleasure devoid of the spiritual. Moreover, as lovemaking is spontaneous, novel and creative, two lovers could not repeat the same experience if they tried. This is why they don't want anyone but their partner. Through the creativity of two people truly making love, they merge into one.

If you grow via romantic love and develop a healthy body, mind and spirit, you may glimpse what sexual ecstasy is all about. Then your sex life will never be the same again.

So how do you decide whether a sexual-skills workshop has value for you? I would challenge you to reflect on your intentions, first and foremost. Is your intention to strengthen the love experience or your sensory experience? Does the effort you're putting in and the time and money you're willing to devote match your intention?

If the instruction you seek will enhance your ability to create intimacy with your partner, then this learning is good. If you want to learn to heighten your sensory experience and that's what your teacher is offering, that's also good.

But if you want to improve the quality of your love through profound sexual intimacy and the program addresses only sensory experience, you may be disappointed. If you want deep emotional and spiritual bonding, what you need to develop are your human qualities: your capacity for commitment, devotion, respect, generosity, caring and sensitivity.

FURTHER CONSIDERATION

- What do you believe are the key differences between sex and passion? Or do they mean the same thing to you?

- Do you feel you invest intention, attention and concentration in your daily activities? In what ways? Do you feel you invest them in your relationship? In what ways? If you don't feel this is a valuable concept, why not?

- Have you experienced qualitative differences in different sexual experiences? If you have, to what would you attribute these differences? For example, did the mental attributes of intention, attention and concentration play a role?

- Given human nature, the sizzling sex in your new relationship will die down sooner or later. How do you and your partner work to keep your relationship sexually alive?

- You know your partner's habitual responses inside out. Does that mean you really know your partner? If not, what should knowing your partner include?

- Do you feel safe with your partner? Do you think your partner feels safe with you? Do you feel there's mutual trust and respect between you? If so, how would you say the two of you have built such qualities? If not, what might you do to change that?

- Do you see a distinction between having sex and making love? How old were you when you began to make this distinction? What caused it? Do you think it's possible to "just have sex" within a true romantic relationship, or have a deeply spiritual sexual experience with someone you are not in a true romantic relationship with?

- Outside of your relationship, what are you passionate about in life? How do you think your life passion ties in with your love relationship?

- How would you define "friend"? Would you say you're friends with your partner? If so, what role does your friendship play in your relationship?

SIX

Suffering for Love: Growing Pains

N AN EPISODE of the popular TV series *Sex and the City*, Carrie Bradshaw, the protagonist, notes that "a relationship without pain is a relationship not worth having. To some, pain implies growth. But how do we know when the growing pains stops and the pain-pains take over?"[1]

The question of how a person knows when enough is enough is a good one and it takes self-awareness and maturity to ask it of ourselves. The object of Carrie's inquiry is her own experiential self, observed in a non-attached way. She wants to understand the nature of pain in relation to her life situation. She also wants to find a solution to her love challenge.

It implies that she does not blame her lover for her pain. Instead, she wants to understand herself by understanding what she is experiencing. With an accurate understanding of the nature of her pain, she can make an informed decision about how to handle the love problem. It takes courage to learn about ourselves, and from the mistakes we make. In American developmental psychologist Jane Loevinger's nine-stage theory of ego, the fifth stage of development is self-awareness. Self-awareness is characterized by what Loevinger calls "increased introspection" with increased awareness that one's own behaviour isn't perfect.[2]

Of course, it's much easier to blame problems in the relationship on our partners. Instead of asking, "What do I need to change?" we ask, "How can I make them change?" This question reveals consciousness that is directed outward. We do not want to know the truth about ourselves and what we bring to the relationship that is contributing to our problems.

Are there existential and/or spiritual reasons behind the pain we experience in a relationship? Friedrich Nietzsche is credited with saying, "If we have our own why in life, we shall get along with almost any how."[3] With that in mind, if we can understand why we suffer in the pursuit of love and happiness, not only can we bear the pain, but we can use it to help us grow.

How you conceive of love and pain depends on your worldview. If you are scientific—if you believe that the main point of human life is to pass our genes on to the next generation—it makes sense that you would look for a partner who will bring only pleasure, no pain. But oftentimes our behaviour defies this logic. It seems we love to torture ourselves by choosing an inconsiderate partner and then voluntarily staying with them well after the pain has become unbearable.

The view of pain in the Abrahamic religions—that is, Judaism, Christianity and Islam—does not seem to make much sense as far as I can see, either. In these religions, an almighty being endows us with the free will to make choices. But if we make morally right choices, we don't necessarily have an easier life. When bad things happen to good people, some believers of these three religions say, "God has his reasons." When those bad things lead to immense suffering they say, "the greater the suffering in this life, the greater the reward in the next."

Yet some people enjoy extreme good fortune in their lives even if they don't make morally good choices. In a relationship context, it seems that some people who try very hard to have a positive, healthy relationship have trouble achieving their goal, while those who are self-centred and ego-driven never seem to get their comeuppance—at least not in this life. It just doesn't seem fair.

From a reincarnation worldview, however, there is a reason we experience pain. We are reborn on this planet over and over again to learn the spiritual lessons we need to learn in order to purify our body, mind and soul, so that when we have finally lived enough lives and learned all our lessons, we can stop the rebirth cycle and return home to love.

This learning is usually triggered by pain. Growth is transformation. In order to be different tomorrow, we must let go of what we were yesterday. This is not easy! Before our harmful attitudes, assumptions and habits can be discarded, they must be challenged, tested and found lacking. Before we can make a lasting change in ourselves, we must feel the need to do so, and that need often comes from experiencing the pain brought upon us by our old ways. In this context, pain and love are the twin catalysts that transform human qualities and consciousness.

In the process of maturation, we expand our sense of self to include our romantic partner. If we choose to create a family with our partner, our sense of self expands to include our children. When we become parents, our feelings for our own parents deepen. After we have reconciled our life conflicts, we grow more inclusive. We include our friends in our sense of self. As we expand our identity, we begin to include our community in our sense of self. From there, we expand our sense of self to include our society, our country, all races, all life forms and ultimately the whole cosmos. And it all grows from the interaction of love and pain.

Herein lies the reason that so many relationships falter. When we are looking for easy rewards, the work necessary to get through the hard parts just doesn't seem worth the effort. Once the needs are no longer being met, there is no reason to stay.

Of course, there are exceptions to this. As we saw in Chapter 4, partners in codependent and dependent relationships may remain in them, unhappily, for a lifetime. But many of us would not stay in a painful or unsatisfying relationship unless we were still in love, because it's love that compels us to remain connected to that person.

In order to grow, we need one or two special love relationships to anchor and ground us in the midst of pain and suffering. This is where the magic of true romantic love comes in, the binding force that prevents us from letting go of this person. In a true romantic-love relationship, the bond is stronger than liking or even loving someone. Even when the going gets tough, the partners are likely to stay longer in an effort to improve their relationship and refine their respective human qualities. The pain and suffering in the relationship propel the couple to change and grow against a backdrop of love. Thus, pain and suffering in a true romantic-love relationship play a crucial function in developmental growth. Without love, the pain of spiritual growth is difficult to endure. Yet without pain, we have no incentive to change.

Why Does Love Hurt?

Pain can be classified in different ways. In this book, I classify pain as physical, socio-psychological or spiritual. Although by some definitions the terms "pain" and "suffering" are quite different, in this book I use them interchangeably.

In the same way that physical pain can alert us to the fact that something may be wrong with our bodies, socio-psychological and spiritual pain inform us that something is hurting our state of being. In this section, I focus on two possible sources of this pain: unmet needs that we want others to meet and our own negative human qualities that harm our sense of self and strain our interactions with others. This is important because when we become aware of what's causing our pain in a relationship, that can help us decide whether to stay or move on.

Psychologist Abraham Maslow developed a well-known theory of a hierarchy of human needs.[4] It comprises five levels of needs, from basic physiological (food, water, warmth, rest) and safety needs (security, safety), to psychological needs for love and belonging (friends and intimate relationships) and self-esteem (sense of accomplishment), and finally self-actualization (achieving one's full potential). According to Maslow's famous theory, one must satisfy the basic survival needs in order to move on to the psychological needs, and from there to self-actualization. In early childhood, basic physiological needs such as food, water, warmth and rest are the most important. Assuming those are adequately met, unmet psychological needs, such as love and a sense of belonging, are the most likely to cause the discomfort and tension we call pain. No matter how loving and skilled our parents were, we almost inevitably emerge from childhood with some damage; that's just a condition of being human. However, assuming the damage is not extreme, and we reach adulthood with a balanced sense of self, then we enter a relationship with an expectation that our partner will work with us to meet each other's needs—a reasonable expectation.

When we are in pain, it is likely that one or more of our needs are not being met. Then we need to ask ourselves who is responsible for creating the pain. In most cases, both partners contribute to creating the pain in the relationship. However, it's possible that one person is contributing more to the problem than the other.

Although Will and Rebecca are attracted to one another when they meet at university, neither is ready for a commitment, so instead of entering a relationship, they become friends. Rebecca is from a working-class background; an aspiring writer, she wants to use words to change the world. After initially failing in her writing career, she gets a job in a factory. But she sticks with her dream and eventually becomes a successful published author.

Will comes from a wealthy family. Although his parents seem psychologically healthy and caring, his life is basically a playground. He does not need to take responsibility, think about his future or consider anyone but himself. Everything in life comes easily to him, especially women. In time, however, vanity, pride, sex, drugs and alcohol corrupt him. He jumps from one relationship to the next and drifts through life with no purpose, turning to Rebecca for support only when he is depressed.

Eventually, they both marry other people. While Will marries a woman who cheats on him, Rebecca settles into a relationship with a man with whom she is not in love but who meets some of her needs. Both Will and Rebecca are lonely and sad but too proud to admit that the people they want most are each other. At the lowest point of their friendship, Rebecca tells Will she still loves him with all her heart but does not like him anymore as he keeps hurting her. She is ready to open her hand and let go of both Will and the relationship.

WILL AND REBECCA have both brought their imperfect personalities into the relationship. Humanistic qualities mess up many relationships. The key is for both partners to recognize the qualities and work on them together. If one person is willing to do the work but the other isn't, or one person is prepared to do more work than the other, the relationship will not result in true romantic love.

Integration of the Self

In youth, some people learn to be *relationship martyrs*. For cultural reasons, this is more common among women, but some men do this, too. To these individuals, true love is about sacrificing their needs to make their partners happy, even if their partners do not attempt to meet their needs in return. Because we tend to seek out situations that reinforce our beliefs, relationship martyrs gravitate toward partners who only take and never give. Naturally, the martyr feels pain when they feel their own needs are not being met. People in this situation have several options: they can try to compel their partner to become more giving; they can stay in the relationship and bear the pain; or they can leave.

Here, I am not advising relationship martyrs on what choice they should make. It takes two people to make a relationship work, and no one can change your partners but themselves. If they refuse to change and your relationship gives you pain, that pain reminds you that you need to care for your own mental, emotional and physical well-being. If you are a relationship martyr, I encourage you to examine your own thoughts and emotions; your emotional fear might be limiting your perception of your options. It takes courage to overcome this to see that there is an option of leaving. When one partner refuses to do their part, leaving is almost always the best option because it offers the potential for you to continue to learn and grow, even if your partner won't or can't. But it can also be extremely painful— sometimes almost unbearably so. The choice is yours to make.

On the other end of the spectrum are those who tend to think of themselves first. This tendency is particularly common in young men. As they grow and mature, they realize they no lon-ger wish to live only for their own interests. They realize that if they don't take some responsibility for their partner's emotional well-being they won't have a relationship, so they begin to take their partner's needs into consideration. This act of including their partner in their subjective reality represents both differen-tiation and integration of the self.

When relationship martyrs begin to grow, they realize that ignoring their own needs and development is not healthy for anyone—themselves or their partner—and that their needs are just as important as anyone's. Putting on your own oxygen mask first in an air-travel emergency is not selfish; it ensures that you will be able to help others by staying alive.

To use the pain of relationship challenges as a catalyst for growth, both partners must take ownership of their contribu-tion to the problem and commit to making a change for the sake of their relationship. If we are courageous enough to take respon-sibility for our own flaws, our growing pains can be productive. But it takes two. If our partner refuses to heal with us, and we decide to stay with them anyway, the pain turns toxic.

Toxic Pain

Toxic pain is pain that is ignored. While true romantic love raises us up and inspires us to work through our growing pains to become a better person, toxic pain makes us worse off. It low-ers us, makes us unhappier, and worsens our dysfunctional personality traits. It creates drama in our life and rigidity in the personality structure. It damages our emotional and moral sen-sitivity and depletes our energy.

The difference between what I call "growing pain" (which stimulates the lover to mature and take responsibility for their own growth in the relationship) and toxic pain has nothing to do with the origins of the pain. Rather, it has to do with how we respond to it. Will we learn and grow from it? Or will we suppress our needs, deny the problem and remain stuck in a miserable situation?

If you are in a similar situation to Rebecca's, have you considered asking, "Should I stay or should I leave?" and, "Am I experiencing toxic pain or growing pain?" The answer to these two questions may be independent of each other—your heart may tell you to stay even though the pain you're experiencing is toxic, or you may leave even though what you experience is a growing pain. The choices we make depend largely on two things: how we define toxic pain and growing pain, and what stage of development we're at.

Growing pain is inextricably linked with true romantic love. True romantic love has the power to transform the lover in the presence of the beloved, and growing pains are one of the ways transformation occurs. As mentioned, the definition of soulmate can include people who hurt us as well as those who bring us bliss.

There are two causes of pain. The most important cause is how we respond to the pain stimulus. The stimulus itself is actually secondary in its importance. This is because reacting to any stimulus involves choices. We cannot blame our partners for the ways we react. And often the way we react determines whether the nature of the pain is toxic or growing. If Eric says something mean to Sandy, Sandy has a choice in how to react. Any pain she suffers as a consequence of her reaction might be growing pain or toxic pain. Her choices may be limited by her level of maturity; for example, if she's in a codependent relationship, she may be functioning at an earlier level of development and unaware of healthier ways to respond. But no matter what she chooses, Eric will only be responsible for his choices and actions, and Sandy will only be responsible for hers. And each of their choices will determine whether the nature of their pain is toxic or growing.

That said, the stimulus itself is also important. Although the nature of the pain Sandy experiences depends on her reaction to the pain stimulus (in this example, a harsh word from Eric), Eric is responsible for saying it. His intention, behaviour and emotions comprise the pain stimulus, and he has a choice in that.

In the reincarnation approach, we're here to learn spiritual lessons, to try to be non-judgmental, forgiving and accepting. To do this, we have to stop assigning blame. We can accept responsibility for our choices and actions, but blaming or judging ourselves will never be productive. Experiencing pain as a path to growth means taking the responsibility to learn from our mistakes. Self-blame gets in the way of learning just as much as blaming others does.

What to Do if You're in an Abusive Relationship

Not assigning blame, whether to ourselves or others, should not blind us to the fact that other people have the same moral and social obligations to us as we do to them. It is as much our moral obligation to expect our partners to uphold their responsibility in the relationship as it is for us to uphold our own. Holding a partner responsible for wrongdoing is not the same as blaming them. If your partner has not lived up to their moral responsibility, it is up to you to decide what you want to do about it, and then follow through.

Let me be clear: If your mind is hijacked by fear—if you are in a relationship with someone who refuses to acknowledge their dysfunction and mend their ways—then you are in an abusive relationship, and you need to get out. In choosing a healthier emotional environment for yourself, your toxic pain may be transformed into growing pain. But remaining in a damaging situation, or trying to do your partner's healing for them, is not growth. This harks back to the distinction I made in Chapter 2 between "being in the now" and "becoming the now." Too often, people think they can escape the toxic pain of an abusive relationship simply by being present, or turning to meditation or other self-soothing activities. You can't, and you shouldn't try.

It is important to let go of the past, but it's not good to use that philosophy as an excuse for never dealing with anything. If your life with your partner has had too many moments of pain without growth, too many emotional injuries, and too few truly good moments, at some point it's necessary to take stock of your past and your present and decide what kind of future you want—to start becoming the now that you know you deserve. Note that it's not enough simply to leave the relationship; you need to examine your experience for the lessons contained within it, and commit to creating a healthier relationship next time. If we fail to learn the lessons that relationship pain is offering us, then life will keep offering us the same lesson again and again.

What Kind of Pain Am I Feeling?

If you're in a painful relationship, ask yourself the following questions to examine how your mind and heart are reacting to the pain:

- Do your heart and mind become hardened like armour when you think of your partner? Or do they become soft and tender?

- Do you close your mind and heart to the suffering of others? Or do you open them wide?

- Do you blame your partner for your state of mind? Or do you clearly see who is responsible for what and take responsibility for yourself?

- Are you only concerned with whether you should stay or move on? Or do you want to know more about yourself, life and love?

- Does the pain from your relationship drag your self-esteem down? Or does it inspire you to take charge of your destiny?

- Does the pain you feel make you judge or hate yourself, your partner and your life? Or does it awaken you and make you reflect on what life, love and relationships are all about?

If your answer for the first question in each of the above six points is yes, you are experiencing toxic pain. If your answer to the second question in the above six points is yes, you are experiencing growing pain.

Toxic pain in your relationship can make you hate your life; growing pain can open your heart to other people's suffering. Toxic pain can drag your self-esteem into a toilet; growing pain can motivate you to take charge of your life. Toxic pain can make you willing to do anything to gain approval and attention; growing pain inspires you to work on developing happiness within. The transformative process of going through growing pain requires you to face the core of your being, to investigate why you are the way you are. The pain can bring you new courage and a new way to objectively assess your partner's human qualities. It can help you decide what you want.

Ironically, when people at the codependent stage of development experience toxic relationship pain, they are more likely to stay in the relationship. They are also more likely to experience love addiction. Low self-esteem causes many love addicts to avoid soulmates who might find beauty in them and help them grow. Living in fear of their own light, they destroy themselves by having relationships with partners who have similar addiction issues or who bring out the worst in them.

When we have love, sex and relationship addiction, we cannot control our behaviour. We become compulsive and obsessive. We use love, sex and relationships to alter our mood. We crave them to fill the void and make us feel high. Love addicts who have not learned anything from a severely broken relationship typically jump quickly into another relationship without allowing themselves enough time to heal and find the wisdom the broken relationship can offer them. Rebound relationship employment reinforces addictive behaviour patterns.

Some people need relationships with two soulmates in a single life. The first one gives them pain that awakens them to grow, and the second one gives them love to heal their wounds. Relationships based on true romantic love can heal us. When we have addiction issues, we need both professional help and help from a soulmate who engages us in a true romantic-love relationship. An authentic love relationship restores our faith in life.

The objective here is not to give advice but to dissect the possible deeper implication of each option you may confront. It might seem like I'm advising you to leave a relationship if you are experiencing toxic pain, and to stay if you're experiencing growing pain. But that's not quite accurate. If you're trying to hold your partner responsible for doing their share and they're not doing it, it could be that the toxic pain is not yours but theirs. It may be that the only way for you to avoid slipping into it with them is to leave. However, if you think it's possible for them to convert their toxic pain into growing pain, you may want to provide them with an opportunity to do so.

The opposite is also true. You may be in a relationship with great potential for growth, but if you are clinging to toxic elements of your personality, you'll probably respond to your relationship in a way that generates toxic pain in you. But if you have some objective awareness of the moral obligations you and your partner have to each other, you might seek professional help to work through your issues and turn your own toxic pain into growing pain—or you might stay in the toxic relationship until you destroy each other, before one or both of you finally move on.

The point is, it's not quite as simple as saying, "If it's growing pain, stay; if it's toxic, leave." Unfortunately, there are no easy answers.

Moving Forward, Together or Apart

So when is enough enough? When should you stay and dig deeper? When should you leave? Unfortunately, amid emotional turmoil, your rational mind is unlikely to trump your heart. Exhausted, with nothing left to give, you stay in a toxic relationship because you keep hoping your partner will turn around soon. On some level, you know your partner is a jerk who's not worth your effort, yet you cannot let go. Somehow, in this state of mind, you must accept your own imperfection without allowing it to turn into self-hatred. Your problem in this situation is not a love problem. It may have more to do with your stage of development and unhealthy attachment patterns. In this case, it is not love you cannot let go of but the pain caused by karmic and current life conditioning. At this point, you should seek professional help to excavate your hidden issues that are getting in the way of your ability to experience true romantic love.

If you are not at the codependent or early dependent stage of development, you can see every relationship has its own time and purpose. Whether you stay or go, you will find peace if you have honestly given everything possible to this relationship with the intention of becoming a better person. It takes effort and time to quiet your mind and answer the questions at the end of this chapter honestly. But ultimately the choice is yours. Not even your God can make it for you. You are the only one who knows when to hang on and when to let go. But the wisdom of true romantic love from your heart and soul can guide you if you open your heart to this power while you are in the midst of pain.

In life and love, pain is inevitable. We don't have a choice in that. But we do have a choice regarding how we react to the pain. We can let it harden us, make us hate our lives, and hate ourselves. Or we can go deep, and find the love within. The answers are inside us, waiting to be discovered.

Zhena Muzyka, author of the 2014 book *Life by the Cup* and tea entrepreneur, writes that "Pain is the messenger of change. It demands that we grow, endure, and heal. Ultimately, pain transforms us and points us to our true north—our calling. Pain is the fire that makes us into diamonds. It pressurizes our rough, unmet, dark angles into glistening reflectors of our soul's light." [5]

Muzyka's quote is insightful and wise. Pain has a purpose in a spiritual journey. We have a choice how to deal with it, especially pain arising from romantic love. We can treat pain as a friend who reminds us to grow, or as an enemy who wants to kill us. If we treat it as a friend, we will embrace it as part of our true romantic-love experience. If we treat it as an enemy, we will avoid it at all costs, and reject the wisdom it holds. In the process, we will also reject the potential for true romantic love.

FURTHER CONSIDERATION

· Would you agree or disagree with the observation that love without pain is not worth having? Why or why not?

· If the function of physical pain is to alert us to something wrong in our bodies, what do you think is the function of other kinds of pain in life? What is the function of pain in relationships?

· Think about some of the times you've had pain in relationships. Describe one occasion when you think it was growing pain, and another when you think it was toxic pain. What are the differences?

· If you were in a relationship that was causing you pain, how would you try to evaluate whether it was growing pains or toxic pain?

• What does letting go of the past mean to you? In what situations might it not be a good idea to let go of the past?

• "Without love, the pain of spiritual growth is difficult to endure. Yet without pain, we have no incentive to change." What does this statement mean to you?

• Say you had a close friend or family member who was struggling to decide whether to stay in a painful relationship or move on, and they asked you how to know when enough was enough. What would you say?

• How do some people use "being in the now" to deal with relationship pain? Why does it often not work out for them? Do you know anyone who's a relationship martyr? What's their partner like?

• "Pain is the fire that makes us into diamonds." What does this mean to you?

• What kind of relationship suffering makes you a better person and what kind of relationship suffering makes you a selfish person?

SEVEN

Addiction, Infidelity and Healing from Heartbreak

Sweating and struggling to catch his breath, Evan wakes up from a recurring bad dream. It's three o'clock in the morning. The rhythm of his wife's breathing reminds him that he is a married man. He wishes he were single so he could be with his co-worker Holly instead. Fantasies of sex with Holly occupy his every waking moment. Evan loves and hates Holly because she plays with his emotions. Evan is in a state of phantom romantic love.

Before he married, Evan went through a string of short-lived love affairs. One lover said he had an attention-grabbing God mentality. Trying to find the right woman on a website, Evan went on dozens of dates, mostly because he did not want to die alone. But he only really wanted a relationship employee who was reliable and did not complain.

The woman Evan eventually married was hard-working, quiet and dependable, but he felt trapped in their marriage, lonelier and emptier than when he was single. He thinks this must just be life. Plagued by self-doubt and low self-esteem, he is constantly jittery and agitated. To redirect his anxiety, he chats with everyone around him. Using chatting to distract himself from his pain, he does not look inward but becomes addicted to flirting. He craves women's sexual attention as a way of proving his worth. Because he is funny, tall, attractive and sexually skilled, many women are drawn to him, and he places more value on his own need for self-worth than on how he affects anyone else in his life, including his wife.

When Evan met Holly, he saw a lot of his own qualities in her and was immediately drawn to her. Attractive, intelligent, sensuous and superb at chatting and flirting, she also craved male attention. Evan openly pursued Holly in the office without shame even though everyone knew he was married, and she welcomed his attention flirted constantly with him without guilt. They talked softly and laughed loudly. Their body language and tone of voice spoke volumes.

Even though Evan is not sleeping with Holly, their relationship is an emotional infidelity to Evan's wife. But Holly tells everyone they're just friends, because she believes infidelity must involve sex.

Although Evan has a love and relationship addiction with Holly, for Holly it is only relationship addiction. She's in love with Gabriel, their ethical and self-disciplined co-worker. Gabriel wants to be with Holly, but he knows her addictive personality would result in a codependent relationship in which Holly would never grow and heal from her pain. He wants to take care of Holly, but he knows his love for her would only be healing if she were to take responsibility for her life and commit to healing her addiction.

Unlike Evan, who cares most about his own interests and needs, Gabriel's interest in Holly's emotional and physical health is truly romantic. To help her grow, Gabriel is firm in saying he will not get involved with her until she makes a commitment to face her addiction and work on her personal growth. He makes it clear that he will only be in a relationship with her if she chooses personal growth for her own benefit, not just for his sake. He knows she'll probably push him away but, because it is true romantic love, he'd rather hurt her honestly than play her addictive game. If she admits her addiction and has a heartfelt relationship with Gabriel, he will go through growing pain together with her and the intimacy will help her recover.

Gabriel reminds Holly that no one can bring her true happiness except herself. After speaking with her, he maintains a quiet distance while waiting to see if she'll change. He knows if she wants to change, she'll come to him to ask for help. It will mean she is ready to grow. If she does not want to make this commitment to herself, she will hang around Evan or other men like him. Because Gabriel's feelings are true love, he will help her even if it takes her decades to come to terms with her addiction. But he also reminds Holly that if she does not get help, he is prepared to let his romantic feelings slide into friendship. If it takes years for Holly to seek help for her relationship addiction, he will play the role of supportive friend in her life. But if by that time he's committed to another woman, he will no longer be willing to be anything more to her than a friend. In other words, although his love for her is unconditional, the role he's willing to play in her life is conditional on her choices and behaviour.

Like most addicts, Holly does not want to admit to her addiction and tells Gabriel to go to hell. Privately, she does not believe she has the beautiful soul Gabriel sees when he looks at her. She feels unlovable. To ease the pain of what she perceives as Gabriel's rejection and abandonment, she seeks Evan's attention. Although she feels some guilt and shame about flirt-ing with a married man, she rationalizes that if his wife doesn't like how emotionally close Evan and Holly are becoming, it's her own fault for not giving him more of what he needs. But even as Holly's feelings of attachment to Evan grow stron-ger, she does not really trust him. Because they are so much alike, she knows he does not really love her. How can he when he doesn't love himself? She knows he is only using his wife to meet his basic need for security. And she knows that if he were to leave his wife and marry her, he would quickly fall out of love with her and move on to someone else.

Why, she wonders, is she always drawn to men like Evan, who don't love themselves, while pushing away men like Gabriel, who do? Holly is afraid to think about her future as she is afraid that it is her fate to be unhappy. To soothe her pain, she spends more time with Evan, believing her attachment to him is a form of brotherly love. Evan believes he feels romantic love for Holly as he has never desired a woman so much. Neither realizes they are addicts.

Their toxic attachment to each other is pathological because the relationship lacks trust, safety and respect, and is moti-vated by loneliness on both sides. Holly represses and denies her feelings for Gabriel to rationalize his rejection of her; Evan needs to repress his shame over his emotional (and later sex-ual) infidelity. Their loneliness is only deepened by the defence mechanisms their mutual lack of trust triggers.

Eventually, Evan's frustration over his unfulfilled sex-ual fantasy leads him to begin flirting with Jane, the married woman next door, to fill the hole in his empty heart. Jane's husband does little to satisfy her emotional and sexual needs, but every time Evan enters her backyard, he makes her laugh and tells her how much he adores her, giving her the attention her husband does not. Since Jane enjoys sex but hates having sex with her husband, she is not only emotionally lonely but sexually needy. When Evan touches her, she feels sexual impulses charging up her neck. It is the spark that she misses in her empty marriage. Before beginning her affair with Evan, Jane devoured erotic romance novels, taking frequent breaks to bring herself to orgasm. With Evan in her life, she hasn't cracked the spine of a book in weeks.

Unlike Holly, who is not aware that infidelity can be emotional as well as sexual, Jane is fully aware that she is playing a role in Evan's infidelity to his wife. She justifies her cheating by focusing on the feelings of companionship and sensual pleasure she's enjoying with him. Her lonely mind interprets the sexual pleasure and excitement as love. But after sex, when she feels lonelier and more depressed than ever before, she experiences deep toxic pain. She does not know why this is happening, only that she cannot bear to walk away from the affair and go back to reading romantic fantasies. When she begins to feel Evan's sexual attention is not enough, she starts going to bars and picking up strangers to help her act out her fantasies.

Evan finally ends his relationship with Jane after she passes a sexually transmitted infection to him. Outraged, she begins thinking of ways to destroy his marriage and she wishes only terrible things for him and his wife. In fact, any time she sees another couple enjoying each other, Jane wishes them a tragic, broken-hearted ending.

Infidelity and Addiction

Throughout most of this book, I have been writing about people with reasonably healthy self-esteem. In this chapter, I wish to address problems experienced by people struggling with love, relationship and sex addictions, because the way they experience love and attachment is very particular. People who are struggling with relationships merely because they're functioning at a lower level of maturity may or may not need counselling to deal with their relationship pain. Even if they do, they won't need addiction counselling. But addicts are different. They are unable to go through a healing process without professional help.

With this in mind, I have four reasons for telling the story of Evan, Holly, Gabriel and Jane. First, I want to show the difference between infidelity caused by addiction and phantom romantic love, which gives rise to toxic pain, and infidelity committed by a mature personality, which gives rise to spiritual awakening, discussed later in this chapter.

Evan's love for Holly is a classic case of phantom romantic love. While he's in relationship employment with his wife, he's head over heels for Holly; she's his soulmate but not a romantic soulmate. The relationship between them illustrates how life uses karmic forces to help us grow. The reason Holly and Evan cross each other's paths in this life is to relearn moral and life lessons that they failed to learn in their previous lives. To restore self-respect and self-love, they need to terminate this relationship. If they don't, they will continue to meet each other in their future lives to pick up where they left off. This law of karma applies to everyone; all of us will continue to run into the same soulmate and experience similar pain until we consciously choose to grow out of our dysfunctional human qualities that cause the pain.

Evan is a love and relationship addict; frightened by deep emotional issues that have dogged him for years, perhaps even since childhood, he escapes his pain by pursuing one love affair after another. If at some point he tires of this relentless cycle, he might become invested in a relationship with an emotionally mature soulmate, which could motivate him to face his addiction and grow spiritually. That said, it's also possible he'd prefer to lose the relationship than experience the pain of dealing with his issues.

Holly also has potential to grow spiritually. Although she doesn't realize that it's possible to be emotionally unfaithful and that she is therefore participating in Evan's emotional infidelity to his wife, that's more a matter of understanding than intent. As far as she understands the concept of adultery, she is not participating in it. And the fact that she's experiencing subconscious guilt and shame arising from the emotional bond she's created with a married man, even though she doesn't understand why, shows that her addiction has not completely silenced her conscience. In addition, even though she's trying to suppress her feelings for Gabriel in the face of his rejection, she still yearns for his love and this, combined with her moral sensitivity, may trigger her to grow later in life. It's as if her conscience is preparing her for the day when she can stop repressing her feelings, start acknowledging and dealing with them, and begin growing into a better person. She is a step ahead of Evan on her spiritual journey, but they are both travelling the same path.

The second point of this story is that infidelity can be emotional without being sexual. Holly thinks that she is not having an affair with Evan because she has not slept with him. In her mind, she and Evan are just close friends with a strong emotional bond, even though there is plenty of sexual energy between them and, subconsciously, she is aware they are using each other in a codependent relationship. She's confusing the toxic cravings of phantom romantic love with healthy bonding, and fails to see the damage their emotional affair is causing to Evan's psychological state. While Evan is obsessing about her, which makes Holly feel good and eases her pain, he's ignoring his marriage, to which he can't devote any energy because he's giving all his attention to Holly. Worse, Holly is oblivious to her role in hurting Evan's wife, who may not know about his philandering yet but who will one day be an emotional casualty of it. In fact, Holly is blaming Evan's wife for a predicament that is in no way her fault.

My third point in telling this story is that I believe we, as a society, need to re-evaluate the way we treat addicts. Like Evan and Holly, Jane is aware that her sexual affair with Evan is frowned on by society, but she sees herself as a victim, which to her justifies any harm she causes to those around her. Addiction is a mental illness, and there's no point in blaming people for being ill. Like many addicts, Evan, Holly and Jane are running away from the truth about themselves. It can take addicts decades to come to terms with their condition and ask for help. Holly is more fortunate than Jane because Holly crosses paths with her soulmate, Gabriel. Many addicts have no one to remind them of the beauty in their souls. Gabriel's response to Holly is the kind of response we should all strive to extend to one another. He offers to help and support her, but when she turns him down, he distances himself from her romantically in order to care for his own needs. He is not selfish. He understands that every addict recovers in their own time. When we understand this, we can accept the addicts' behaviour gracefully and without judgment, take care of ourselves, and move on.

The fourth reason for telling the story is to help you understand and identify with the characters by seeing yourself or someone you know in them. To grow requires awareness, and most importantly self-awareness. Many people are not aware they have love, sex and relationship addiction; both Evan and Holly are addicted to chatting but rationalize that they are extroverts who love social conversation. Chatting is their way of acting out to avoid the pain of disconnection with themselves. Why should Holly and Evan change if they think their addictive behaviour is just the way they are?

We cannot act to change if we are not aware that we are mentally ill. We need to be educated in the differences between positive and negative mental and emotional health, and to be aware of whether we have an addiction issue. If we are aware we have an addiction issue, we need to confront the truth about ourselves. Being an addict is nothing to be ashamed of; addiction can be healed if we ask for help from our loved ones and professionals.

Usually it is necessary to have help from professionals to assist the recovery journey. The most important thing is to begin the journey by reaching out to people who care about us.

Because addiction is so prevalent, there is a good chance we will cross paths with addicts in our relationships. With awareness, we know how to manage the relationship, as Gabriel does with Holly. More so, when we understand addiction and know that the behaviour of an addict is not who they truly are, it is easier to accept them.

This is not an easy topic for me to write about because I speak from personal experience. Both of my sisters' husbands cheated on them, and one brother-in-law's infidelity directly contributed to my sister's premature death before she turned 40. It was devastating for me to lose her, and I hated my brother-in-law for a long time. But that experience also led me to a deep interest in understanding addiction later in my life, so something positive came out of it. Without my awareness of addiction, it would be difficult for me to learn how to forgive and accept addicts who commit adultery. This personal struggle makes me realize it's important that we understand, as a society, why some people do this and how we can help them, as that is the only way we will ever help the people they hurt.

I do not believe that addiction is only the addict's problem, or that broken romantic relationships are only the individual's psychological challenge. As I discussed in Chapter 2, I believe they are pervasive social problems that impact everyone in the world directly or indirectly. One of my purposes in writing this book is to raise awareness of this belief. I discuss my thoughts on this in more detail in the Epilogue.

Infidelity and Moral Growth

Sex is a natural human activity, but it is loaded with societal and cultural values and beliefs. As long as two people clearly understand the rules of their sexual activity—whether it is a one-night stand, a friendship with benefits, a monogamous relationship or an open relationship—whatever attitude a couple has toward sex is their own business.

That said, I believe there are three levels of morality: legal, conventional and conscience-guided morality.

The first two—that is, laws enacted by legislative institutions and cultural beliefs agreed on by members of a community, reflect collective values. From a North American cultural perspective, adultery transgresses these collective values and social norms. However, those who follow legal and social conventions are not automatically better or more ethical people than those who do not. They are simply observing the rules of a game. If you want to play a game without being called out by the referee, you learn and follow the rules. But rules are human constructs, which means they are not perfect, and sometimes should be challenged.

Infidelity hits at the most fundamental fabric of human relationships and the core of spirituality. How we connect with others is the most important spiritual lesson we need to learn in our lives on Earth. But infidelity destroys multiple connections. When a person cheats, their connection with themselves is damaged by their guilt and shame, which erodes their self-esteem. Their connection with the person they're cheating on is damaged because it erodes the trust between them, and if the other moves on to another relationship it may erode their ability to trust their new partner. And the connection with the person with whom they are cheating is unhealthy, because it's impossible to form an honest relationship from one that is grounded in dishonesty. With all these damaged connections, we lose faith in and disconnect from life itself.

Although I have never been unfaithful, I can imagine how agonizing my guilt might feel for creating in my partner a sense of sexual betrayal or abandonment. Committing adultery would not only strike at the core of the identity that I had created with my partner, but would cause me to question who I am and why I did this to myself and the person I was supposed to care about most.

Our personal sense of right and wrong is not based on laws or conventions but on our psychic capacity to directly feel other people's pain and joy. It is possible for any of us to do what's legally and conventionally right while deep down in our hearts knowing we have hurt someone we loved.

If you are engaging in infidelity or are tempted by it, ask what spiritual lesson you are supposed to learn and how you can grow from it. This is my approach in this chapter—using your conscience as a life compass to tell right from wrong, and to grow from the pain caused by infidelity.

Toxic Adultery vs. Love Triangles

Life is wise. It finds ways to push us to grow. Adultery can be one of those ways. There may be a positive element in the adulterous experience if the cheaters use their feelings of guilt and shame to reflect more deeply on the meaning of love, relationships, life, who they are and why they cheat. If they listen to their hearts, where the conscience resides, they will know whether they're doing the right thing.

Spirituality is about awakening to your true potential and the uniqueness of your ego-self. Identities at earlier stages of development are constructed by our unconscious acceptance of prevailing law, conventional morality and culturally approved values. In these early stages, we act not in a conscious way but an unconscious, conditioned way. We don't examine our beliefs and value systems, or ask questions about who we are and how we became this way.

But spiritual growth challenges one's moral values and beliefs. This questioning can turn into a vehicle for spiritual awakening, a questioning of "Who am I?" and a desire to become a better person by following one's conscience.

Infidelity can be an opportunity for spiritual growth. Let's take the example of Moira, a woman who was lucky enough to find her significant other, Cliff, at a young age. However, amid the couple's happiness and contentment, Moira came to feel an emptiness. Years into their marriage, after they've had two beautiful children, she takes one of her annual trips to a nearby city. On the first day of her vacation, she meets a man, Rob, and, after several drinks, they spend the night together. Their affair continues for the next three days. It is more than just sex. As Moira's vacation nears its end, Rob asks her to run away with him. Although she struggles with the decision, in the end, she returns to her family.

Prior to this incident, Moira had never had to face such a fundamental question of who she is. Sex plays a significant role in this story. Without it, there would no adultery, no moral struggle, and no opportunity for Moira to grow into a better person. But sometimes, life takes us into uncharted territory that forces us to face who we truly are. With a new sense of self, we are forced to make an existential choice regarding what to do with our old lives. This, of course, will have an impact on our spouses and children. This dilemma involves not only moral judgment, but also the nature of true romantic love—to transform oneself in the presence of the beloved.

To understand Moira's dilemma, we need to know a bit more about who she was when she met Cliff. She grew up in a very small town. An only child, her immigrant parents died in a car accident when she was just 18. They left her no money and no family to turn to. Lacking opportunities, she stayed in her small hometown and worked as a waitress at the local diner. That was where she met Cliff. A returning Afghan war vet who was figuring out what he wanted next, he seemed worldly, wise and able to care for her. They married six months later and soon after began their family.

Moira never questioned her life until she was faced with the choice to stay or leave her family at the end of her three-day fling. Many people don't question their lives until they face the possible breakup of a long-term relationship. At this point, she realized how much she valued the way her family anchored her. She'd never had any career plans, but found purpose and meaning in the role of mother and wife. She honestly loves her husband and her family. Her needs are met. She is content. She calls this love—at least until she meets her lover, Rob.

Unlike Evan, Jane or Holly, Moira is not a dysfunctional woman filled with sexual and romantic fantasies. She is dependable and trustworthy. So how to explain her affair? A necessary condition is the existential emptiness she feels. Despite having everything she thought she wanted in life, she feels something is missing. An environmental activist, Rob leads a life of travel and adventure. Except for her annual trips, Moira never leaves her hometown. Rob represents an opportunity for her to step away from her robotic life and live in a way she's only imagined. For his part, Rob is drawn to the calm of her small-town personality and sees a woman who could provide the stability that's been notably missing from his existence. They both have something new and different to offer the other.

Although she struggles with the decision of whether to go away with Rob, in the end she returns to her family. But her decision is not motivated by guilt or fear of the unknown. Nor is she afraid of making a mistake, or of the cost of walking out on her family.

Instead, the affair prompts her to question the meaning and purpose of her life. She experiences a shift: from a woman who has been ruled by her conditioning to an individual making conscious choices about how to live her life. She has always been a good wife and mother, but she didn't really have any choice. After her encounter with Rob, she is determined to take a more active role in the life she's chosen, rather than just going through the motions. Outwardly, nothing has changed; inwardly, everything has.

Once settled back into her old life, she befriends a neighbour who'd been exposed for having an affair and treated as an outcast by most of the town folk because of her adultery. In her conservative community, Moira also joins a forward-thinking environmental group and begins challenging people in her circle to live more thoughtfully. Unashamed finally, she tells her husband about the affair, emphasizing that although she's sorry for any pain she's caused, she's not sorry it happened because she knows it's made her a better person, and that, in turn, will help her children, her husband, her neighbours and her town to be better.

It would be nice if all adulterous affairs could end on such a positive note, but for the most part they end messily. Everyone in the adulterous triangle is hurt, as are the children, other family members and possibly friends. Is there any way for all parties in the adulterous relationship to learn and grow?

Healing from Infidelity

We are here to learn the life and love lessons we need to complete our spiritual journey. Growth involves pain. If we see pain and loss as the price we need to pay for growth, then pain from all experiences including infidelity is bearable and can be meaningful. We will not be judged on whether we committed adultery, but on how pure the quality of love we experienced in adultery was, and how ethically we treated the people involved. There is no judgment day in the reincarnation worldview. God can take a permanent vacation. The law of karma may send adulterers to heaven and non-adulterers to hell, assuming such places exist.

In discussing recovery and possible growth from infidelity, it's important to understand the role played by the developmental stage. Returning to our story about Evan, Jane and Holly, Evan is clearly at the codependent stage. His capacity to feel his own and other people's pain is distorted. Because he does not take responsibility, his morality is also compromised. As Evan is in a codependent marriage with a wife who is likely also codependent, it is unlikely he will grow spiritually from infidelity. Individuals must be at least aware enough to be at the dependent stage in order to use infidelity as a springboard for spiritual growth.

Holly and Jane are also codependent. However, Holly seems to have some self-awareness. Recognizing that she and Evan are similar in personality and addictive traits, she knows enough not to trust him. This is the kind of dispassionate self-assessment that's only available to us at the dependent stage. And if she's at the dependent stage, and has Gabriel's support, it's possible she could grow to the independent stage in this lifetime. Jane may need new stimulus to help her to look inward to her state of mind. She is stuck but her moment of awakening may come.

The cost of infidelity is the emotional pain caused by betrayal. This triggers issues of safety and trust, which are the bedrock of a healthy relationship. But the most damaging effect is the ethical dimension of cheating. In an adulterous triangle, all three players are likely to feel guilt and shame. The offender feels guilt and shame for damaging their partner's trust in them. The co-offender feels guilt and shame for contributing to hurting the offender's partner and possibly damaging their relationship. And even the one who is offended against might feel guilt and shame, perhaps blaming themselves for doing something to bring it on or simply feeling ashamed that somehow they didn't know about the infidelity. So how can they each approach this painful situation in a way that will bring wisdom and expanded awareness to minimize trauma, heal their pain and accelerate their spiritual growth?

One practice in traditional Chinese medicine is to use small doses of poison mixed with other herbs to cure a patient's ailments. Similarly, in the situation of infidelity we can use pain to cure pain and then use it further to accelerate spiritual growth and healing, but there are differences in how each member of the adulterous triangle will do this.

Adulterer and Co-adulterer

If the adulterer and the co-adulterer are morally sensitive and responsible, cheating will be an excruciatingly painful experience for both. Because they violate their own moral code, they feel lost. However, there must be a reason they risked their sense of self-worth and paid such a hefty price to experience the romantic liaison. It is likely that there is an important spiritual/humanistic lesson that both need to learn, and the lesson may also involve the victim. Whether the adulterer and the spouse decide to get back together or to dissolve the relationship, they need to ask themselves why they became a couple in the first place—were they in true romantic love and they fell out of love, or was their union a case of relationship employment? Further, this lesson may have originated from their past lives and carried over to the current life. A couples' therapist may be able to help both partners find the answers, and the spiritual wisdom within the infidelity.

Healing is about returning to wholeness. Guilt and shame are two different moral emotions. Guilt is about a person's behaviour violating their own moral code, whereas shame is a negative evaluation of their own worth. When we mature, the socio-psychological emotions of guilt and shame originate from our conscience, which enables us to intuitively differentiate right from wrong.

There is a difference between love and true love. Caring for others is easy when life is good. It is only when things are not going well that we learn the true capacity of our love. True love occurs when we maintain love for others and ourselves when we are in pain and we feel everyone is betraying us. Only in pain do we discover if our love is genuine. The love lesson in infidelity is to learn to forgive and accept non-judgmentally while you are in pain.

For the adulterer and co-adulterer, guilt and shame are positive insofar as they act as reminders to grow and change to avoid hurting loved ones in the same way ever again. When we heed these reminders, our damaged self-esteem begins to recover, whereas if we ignore our conscience, these two emotions remain with us, transforming into a toxic stew that further corrodes our self-esteem and leads us into addiction.

The healing process involves rebuilding faith and trust in ourselves. This is the lesson we must learn, and we do this by being non-judgmental and accepting of who we are, and forgiving ourselves for what we did. This is one of the hardest spiritual lessons we will ever have to grapple with.

If both adulterer and co-adulterer are morally sensitive people, they will not want to go through this painful ordeal. Yet a tremendous energy may be pulling them together so strongly that they cannot resist. Although they know they have a choice, their rational minds cannot stop them.

Think of this metaphor. If you are driving your car at high speed, it will take much more effort, time and distance to stop than if you are driving slowly. If a romantic attraction carried over from a past life mixes with current life conditions—for instance, an empty and dull marriage without love—the force of attraction will be equivalent to a high-speed joyride.

Even though you try to brake the car, you may not stop, as the force is too powerful for your volitional mind and conscience to intervene. What I am trying to say here is that some affairs have their own karmic forces. People can experience karmic consequences from both past and current lives, forces that are stronger than we can manage. But if we use the pain from our guilt and shame to redeem ourselves, then there is nothing to be ashamed of. We are all humans. With the exception of a few advanced spiritual leaders, we return to this Earth plane to learn and grow. Becoming involved in this kind of affair is not a mistake even though the volitional mind and society disapprove. It is a spiritual lesson that the adulterer and their partner need to learn.

Victim

The healing challenge for the victim of an adulterous triangle is that they feel like, well, a victim. A victim mentality thwarts healing and growth. Victims rarely want to understand the motives of the people who destroyed their family, life and stability. Victims must allow themselves time to heal from this pain and go through the necessary emotional cycles. At this stage, victims are wise to seek professional help. They must cool down before doing their spiritual work. It is important for the victim to honour their own emotions before attempting any spiritual growth. It dishonours the self to offer forgiveness prematurely, while ignoring our own profound pain. You do not have to be superhuman. You need to go through your own emotional process as part of healing. Please honour whatever emotion comes into your consciousness before you start thinking about how to forgive and accept. Remember that anger is pain in disguise. It's okay to feel it and express it.

Once they have processed their emotions, the wronged party may be able to find the inner resources to move forward with nonjudgmental acceptance and forgiveness. The key is empathetic understanding of themselves, their partnership with the adulterer, and the adulterous couple. In this moment, the victim needs to find the courage to learn the spiritual wisdom of infidelity. The victim's emotional pain stems from the challenge to their sense of self-worth. The infidelity fills them with self-doubt. Yet, the most important source of pain is the breach of trust. They married their partner believing that person had their best interest at heart. They trusted their partner to protect and care for them. Their partner's infidelity shattered that trust and destroyed their sense of safety. With their ability to trust or feel safe with anyone severely damaged, the victim loses faith in life. Some victims become extra vigilant and cannot open their hearts to trust anyone. Some are never able to love again. In this state of mind, how can the victim grow spiritually and heal the pain?

At this point, the victim must remember that there is still one person they can trust: themselves. It might be true that, in that person's experience, no one follows through on their promises. Perhaps everyone the victim knows looks out only for their own self-interest. They can control no one but themselves, so that's what they must do.

Earlier, I pointed out that although we may not be able to control the source of pain, we can control our reaction. The victim has the power to control how they respond to this ordeal and what kind of person they want to be. Because the victim has a first-person experience of how deeply their partner's infidelity hurts, they might vow never to inflict similar pain on anyone else. Moreover, the tenderness in the victim's heart might enable them to feel greater empathy for others in the same situation. The victim can transform their pain into love. In the process of healing from the pain, they become a better person. And in the process of becoming a better person, their faith in life is restored. From then on, no one can take that faith away because the victim—now the survivor—knows they have full control. Moreover, because the survivor now understands the pain has a deeper purpose, they can endure it with grace.

I know my suggestions for healing are not easy. It is a lot easier to find peace while sitting in meditation and experiencing the serenity of stillness than when you are in pain and chaos. And I stress again that you must give yourself time to get through your anger and pain, to deal with your emotions as they arise, before you start trying to grow. Experiencing your emotions as they are is a vital part of the healing process.

But you can't allow yourself to dwell in your emotions forever because you cannot grow in this state. To grow, we need to confront the shadow that has been awakened by the pain. This is when you find out who you are and how much spiritual work you need to do.

That said, spiritual recovery, healing and growth require training and knowledge. Applying this knowledge in a sort of how-to manner really requires working with a good therapist or life coach. Reading this book and watching spiritual videos on YouTube won't be enough. The way you see things can change in an instant, but it can take years of work to recognize that instant when it happens. And the earlier your stage of development, the more likely you're going to need help.

"Conscious Uncoupling"

Infidelity is not the only reason for a relationship to end. Another difficult situation occurs when one partner feels compelled to leave one relationship for another, but wishes to do this with grace, dignity, and respect for the other partner's feelings—to do it without "cheating" at all.

When two people enter a relationship, they bind themselves to each other emotionally, energetically and often materially through a shared home or possessions. Dissolving those bonds can be painful because it means disconnecting from a person who was once part of you. This is one reason why separating a household is so difficult. It isn't dividing the dishes that's upsetting; it's the fact that you will no longer eat off them together.

Because this discomfort is so hard to face, many people stay in relationships that have run their course long past the point when their hearts tell them it's time to move on. But ignoring the heart's call to move on can breed frustration, resentment and intolerance. It can lead one or both partners to manufacture a crisis, such as an affair, to use as an escape hatch. While this often succeeds in ending the relationship, it is also likely to traumatize both people, and the trauma can easily spread to the new relationship, as well.

Affairs are painful because one partner is giving special attention to someone outside of the relationship, and because they have lied or hidden something important from their partner. If you feel you need to leave your partner for someone else, and you're already giving special attention to someone new, you can't change the fact that your partner will be hurt by this. But you can minimize the pain of rejection for them by telling them about the new lover as soon as possible rather than making them feel they've been deceived, by being honest about why you're leaving, resisting any impulse to blame them, yourself or the new lover, and by minimizing contact with your new lover until your physical separation is complete.

This last point is important to ensure you're not exacerbating your old partner's trauma by waving your new love in their face. For example, if you are still living with your old partner, you and your new partner might agree to only talk on the phone when you know your old partner will not be within earshot. You can choose not to go away for a romantic weekend together until you've physically moved out. At the very least, you can agree not to have sex with your new lover until you have physically separated from your old partner.

You can also make sure you're not giving your old lover mixed messages. One of the most difficult aspects of ending a relationship can be the fear of losing the friendship underlying the sexual relationship. This will be particularly so in a true romantic-love relationship, where a passionate love has been built on a foundation of passionate friendship. But many couples try to rush a post-separation friendship by failing to have a period of conscious physical separation, which provides a sort of buffer zone in which both partners, and particularly the one who is being left, can reimagine and reconfigure their daily lives. Without this period of time, couples can slip back into habits like watching TV together or walking the dog together, which can unfairly lull the partner who is being left into believing the relationship is on the mend. Sometimes, to guard against this slipping, one of the partners will regress into anger, blame and recrimination, which will only deepen the trauma of separation for both old partners and, possibly, the new lover as well.

PARTNERSHIPS END FOR many reasons, and not all of them involve a third party. Perhaps the two individuals have learned all they can from one another. Perhaps one person is growing more quickly than the other, and needs to be with someone who can meet and challenge them at a new level. Perhaps they have simply grown apart and yearn for new experiences. It is far more likely for partners at a mature stage of development and in a true romantic-love relationship to choose to leave a relationship without the appearance of a third party than it would be for partners at an earlier stage of development.

Regardless of their cause, breakups are rarely easy. But they do not need to be devastating, either. The emotional and spiritual maturity that come with true romantic love can make it possible for partners to act with grace and dignity for the sake of all concerned, even while ending a relationship. That doesn't mean no one will feel hurt. However, an open-hearted, responsible breakup guided by love can reduce the intensity of the pain, and allow everyone the best chance of moving through the transition with their hearts and maybe even their friendship intact, as we will see with Bev and Abby's story.

Abby and Bev had been seeing each other for just over three years when Bev decided she needed to be single again. From Abby's perspective, the timing could not have been worse. She had just left her job to launch a new business, and was counting on Bev for emotional and practical support.

Although they had not yet lived together, Abby had been hoping that might change, especially since her teenage daughter would be leaving for university soon. She was enthusiastically looking forward to building a life with Bev, whom she considered the kindest person she had ever met.

A deeply empathic person, Bev always seemed to know exactly what Abby was feeling and why. Abby had never felt as safe and understood as she did with Bev. Their relationship was emotionally warm and physically passionate. They enjoyed abundant laughter and great sex, and had a wide circle of friends who all got along with one another. Abby had wanted that feeling to last forever, and even hoped to marry Bev one day.

In the early days of their relationship, they had both enjoyed indulging in fantasies of domesticity. Should Abby move into Bev's rural retreat, or would Bev move into Abby's city flat? But, about six months before the breakup, Abby noticed that this conversation seemed to put Bev on edge. Instead of talking about the future in terms of "we" and "ours," Bev increasingly spoke about "my plans" for long solo journeys in the wilderness. This pushed Abby's panic buttons, causing her to demand more and more reassurance that the relationship was secure, which in turn pushed Bev further and further away. Abby, who had been a single parent for years, was ready for a serious commitment. Bev, who had rolled right into a relationship with Abby after coming out of a long-term partnership, had a powerful need for freedom.

It would have been easy for Bev to have an affair. Attractive to both men and women, she was constantly being propositioned. But she didn't want to put either of them through the drama of infidelity and heartbreak. Bev had stayed too long in her last relationship, growing restless and discontent, eventually leaving her wife only after she met Abby. It had been a painful and embarrassing experience for everyone, and she had no desire to play the "bad guy" again.

The three weeks that followed Bev's admission that she no longer wanted to be in a committed relationship with Abby were tearful and intense. The couple decided not to see each other for a while, and also not to talk about their situation with their friends, which would surely only inflame emotions and create conflict between them. While they were apart, Abby realized that although she was hurt, she wasn't angry, because Bev really hadn't done anything wrong. She had simply chosen a different path, and expressed her decision in a kind and respectful way.

Abby was sad, very sad, to lose her lover, but what she feared most was losing Bev from her life altogether. She didn't want their friends to have to pick sides. She didn't want to have to avoid each other at group events. She didn't want their happy memories to be tainted by bitterness. More than anything, she didn't want to lose access to Bev's loving friendship. Bev felt the same way.

When they were ready, they met at Bev's country house, built a big fire in the wood stove, cried, held each other, and jointly let the relationship go. Or rather, they kept the relationship, but changed its parameters. They would not be lovers anymore. They would not be life partners. They would go their separate ways and pursue their own dreams. But they promised that they would still be able to call on one another in times of need or celebration, and vowed to take each other up on that.

There were more tears after that, but both women were surprised by how relatively cleanly and quickly the pain washed away. The vessel for their relationship had changed shape, but it was still intact, and the love inside was pure and unpolluted.

Shortly after their "conscious uncoupling"—a term coined by marriage therapist Katherine Woodward Thomas and popularized by divorcing celebrity couple Gwyneth Paltrow and Chris Martin—both women met new partners, and both were glad they had created space in their lives for these new people to come in without conflict or compromise. Three years after ending their romantic relationship, Bev was a guest at Abby's wedding to her new partner.

One Partner or Many?

As we encounter multiple soulmates in each lifetime, we don't form romantic attachments with all of them. Some come into our lives at the wrong time, such as when we are already in a relationship; even though we feel drawn to them, we are not open to becoming romantically involved with them. Others may be incarnated as family members.

It's possible to learn one lesson with one soulmate, and different lessons with another soulmate. Thus, we could potentially have several partners in a lifetime, and they could all be our soulmates. How do we know if a person we have just met is the one we are waiting for? As mentioned, this depends on our psychic sensitivity and stage of development. A few of us feel early on in a relationship that a certain person is the only one for us in this life (as with "love at first sight"). But many of us do not know which romantic relationship is the most important until we are near the end of our life journey.

In today's fast-paced, stressful society, emotions are easily aroused. In Western culture, women and men can easily meet and create relationships in different life situations. With so many opportunities, it is easy to cross paths with soulmates or new souls who arouse our romantic interest unintentionally. Here are two possible ways to handle an unexpected romantic challenge.

First, if we cannot have sex with a certain potential romantic partner, we feel incomplete, isolated and distant. But if we are already in a committed relationship, having sex with this soulmate is adultery. If we are able, we can transform our sexual passion into the enduring life passion of beautiful friendship. Does the absence of sex mean the struggle with our romantic soulmate is not romantic love? Remember, the definition of true romantic love is the power to make the lover want to be a better person in the presence of the beloved. To sublimate and transform a potentially romantic relationship into a beautiful friendship requires true maturity and potentially challenges the couple to even more spiritual growth than if they were to explore sexual union.

Second, if we choose to let go of the current relationship and pursue the new relationship, we need to deal with it ethically. We might choose not to lie to our partner. We might exit the relationship we're in before we have sex with the new person. It's not painless, but it's also not "infidelity" or betrayal.

Unrequited Love

It is possible to transform unrequited romantic love into true romantic love if both members of the couple are mature enough.

Consider Rose, who is madly in love with John. John feels he and Rose are soulmates, but not in a sexual way. Feeling rejected, Rose asks herself what she really wants with John. If she simply wants to make him happy, she can still do so as a friend. As John's friend, Rose gives unconditional regard and financial support to John's artistic venture.

How can John tell if his friend's love for him is an addictive attachment? The true test comes when John finds happiness in a relationship with another woman. If Rose has an immature, addictive personality, she might lose control of her behaviour and even start stalking him. If Rose has a balanced, mature personality, and her love for John is true romantic love, she will be hurt but at the same time feel truly happy for him. However, if she's also wise, she will not push herself to see if she can attain superhuman maturity by remaining in a situation that's hurtful.

Once it becomes clear that John will never be interested in anything more than friendship, and that Rose will have to abide his relationship with his new love, it is up to her to maintain a proper distance as a friend so that John's new lover will not feel threatened by her presence in John's life. Rose may need to take a breather from John to heal. There's nothing wrong with that.

However, true love will prevail if this experience serves to help Rose become a better person. Deep down, what she wants most is to see John happy. She transforms her affection from that of a lover to that of a mother. When she regards John as more of a son, she is happy to see that he is happy with another woman. Likewise, if Holly were to go back to Gabriel for help even after he enters into a relationship with another woman, accepting his new girlfriend would be part of her maturation process. This is the transformative power of true romantic love. We may switch from one role to another, but the love continues.

In an unrequited love situation, one of the most difficult challenges is to avoid trying to make the other person feel guilty. It can be particularly hard to resist the impulse to turn hurt into anger or inappropriate behaviour. It requires a high level of maturity to use unrequited love as an opportunity to become a better person. In most cases, we may need to distance ourselves from our object of unrequited love in order to heal from the pain of rejection.

Feelings are feelings. There is no right or wrong about them. For most of us, spiritual growth means recognizing how we feel and then taking steps to protect ourselves from unnecessary pain. The sentiment you experience makes you who you are. Denying your feelings is likely to lead you to unhealthy thoughts, and possibly actions, and this is likely to interfere with your present and future spiritual development. By accepting your emotional state and working with it, you are far more likely to be able to transform your painful experience into the kind of growth that empowers you to become a better human.

Life is an interplay of two forces called yin (feminine) and yang (masculine). In the Chinese tai chi symbol, the yin area has a dot of yang and the yang area has a dot of yin. The stories of awakening adultery in this chapter illustrate this life principle. In negativity, we find the silver lining of the human goodness. In positivity, we find a seed of corruption. This is life.

I don't want to mislead you into thinking we should let go of human-made morality. Communities cannot function without rules and laws. The problem is not human-made rules and laws but the human qualities that create and enact those rules and laws. Rules and laws are meant to be changed as time passes. Knowing when to let go and when to hold onto past wisdom is a challenge to the individual and collective consciousness. We learn from our collective mistakes together.

There are many ways to heal from heartbreak, whether it's caused by relationship addiction, infidelity, unrequited love or any other painful type of relationship dynamic. Sometimes, the pain is so intense that we must seek help in recovering from it, but we can only use our individual judgment regarding when and what kind of help to seek. It is particularly important for male readers to open themselves to seeking help after a romantic breakup, as the average man tends to be less emotionally expressive than the average woman.

That said, the best healing modality is prevention. Life has ups and downs, and loss is part of life. Romantic heartbreak offers us opportunities to learn about ourselves and life. This does not mean that we should venture into the romantic arena recklessly. If you know your romantic imagination can be easily aroused, you need to find ways to protect yourself. Moreover, if you are aware that your personality includes borderline addictive tendencies, you need to find ways to protect yourself emotionally and psychologically to prevent spiralling further downward.

Whatever romantic ups and downs life brings you, the most effective tool for healing after heartbreak is to find aspects of the painful experience that can help you grow and improve your self-awareness. We can't avoid growing pains in life, but we can prevent growing pain from becoming toxic pain.

FURTHER CONSIDERATION

- When you are lonely, or feel empty or anxious, how do you distract yourself from these feelings? Under what circumstances do you think these behaviours might become addictions?

- How might you tell the difference between healthy romantic bonding and addictive cravings in yourself? In a friend? In a romantic interest?

- What do you think about the idea that addiction is not a moral issue because addicts cannot control the behaviours that harm others? Does your opinion change if you think about an addictive behaviour in yourself or a loved one, as opposed to a similar behaviour in a total stranger?

- What is your moral belief about infidelity? For example, do you think it's always wrong, no exceptions? Do you think there might sometimes be good reasons for infidelity? If so, what do you think some such reasons might be? If not, why not? Are there any circumstances in which you think relationships and individuals can grow as a result of infidelity?

- What do you think the long-term consequences might be of repressing a guilty conscience caused by infidelity? How might a person use their guilt and shame to grow? How might they amend the wrong they've done?

- The text suggests that emotional intimacy outside a long-term relationship is a form of infidelity. Do you agree? Why or why not? If your answer would vary in different situations, explain.

- Have you ever played a role in an adulterous relationship, whether as adulterer, co-adulterer or victim? If so, what did this experience (or these experiences) teach you about yourself?

- Imagine you are in a situation of unrequited love. How might you go about cultivating an intimate friendship with the object of your affection without crossing the line into inappropriate and unwanted behaviours?

- What are the key factors in ending a relationship with as little trauma and heartbreak as possible? Reflecting on your breakups, have you behaved in ways you later regretted? Have you also behaved at times in ways you feel helped you to grow emotionally and spiritually?

EIGHT

Transforming Your Relationship into True Romantic Love

Max examines the coffee cup in his hands as if it contains the answers to the mysteries of the universe. A gust of wind blows dry leaves across the path in front of the park bench where he sits, but he doesn't raise his collar against the chill. All he can think about is the remarkable conversation he had with Emily the previous night.

He feels as though he is sitting on a volcano about to erupt. What is this mix of emotion? Nervousness, certainly. Confusion. Perhaps some skepticism. Disbelief. But underneath all of that is a quietly powerful feeling that he finds difficult to pinpoint, let alone name.

Max searches for the words to describe it. Joy is part of it, but it's more than that. There is also relief, and something like the opposite of disillusionment. It's the feeling you get *returning home after a long and difficult journey, when you put your key in the lock and set your bags down in the hall. The hairs on Max's neck stand on end as he realizes he hasn't had this feeling for a very long time, if ever: sanctuary.*

Max has been single for most of his 47 years. Of course he has dated women—quite a few, in fact. But since leaving his first wife at 29, he has not stayed with anyone longer than a few months. For Max, relationships have been a game of cat-and-mouse, or maybe a gladiatorial battle. Romance has always been about power: who had more and how they used it to control the other person. Max never discussed this with his girlfriends, and barely articulated it to himself, but he could tell from their actions they were playing the same game.

His relationships always started out with flirtation, followed by mutual seduction. Sooner or later, they'd go to bed together. Then one of them would have the first bad mood, the other would withdraw or lash out, and it would go downhill from there. Max is tired of this game. It's fun to date someone new, but it's also exhausting and, recently, it's been getting dull.

With Emily, the first bad mood was his. As usual, he and Emily had been working hard to impress each other and each had put on an attractive persona in the six weeks they'd been seeing each other. The previous night, however, he was feeling tense and took it out on her over dinner. He blamed his tension on a difficult day at work, but if he's honest, it stemmed from a subject that Emily had brought up—the upcoming holidays. Her sister was coming to town for Christmas, and Emily was looking forward to it. In Max's experience, women talking about holidays was always followed by a lot of guilt trips and passive-aggressive pressure, either to come meet their family, or to take them away from it all on a tropical vacation.

If there's one thing Max can't stand it's feeling manipulated. Because it's late October, he's been fully expecting the subject *of the holidays to come up, so when Emily mentioned it, he immediately thought "Here we go," and his mood subtly soured. For the next hour he teased her and tossed veiled insults at her, playfully at first, then with increasing hostility and irritation.*

Emily's response surprised him. Instead of jabbing back at him as he expected her to do, she called his bluff. "Ouch," she said to one of his so-called jokes. "That was a little harsh." Looking him in the eyes, she placed one hand on the table between them. She said she had noticed something had changed in him around the time the salads were served, and asked what he was thinking about. At first he denied anything was wrong and suggested that maybe she was the one with the problem. But she didn't take the bait. "Was it because I brought up Christmas? You don't have to come for dinner, you know. In fact, I'm not really ready for that either." Max's relief was apparent. Rather than turning it into an issue, Emily laughed sympathetically, and said that it sounded like he'd been what she called a "Christmas casualty" before.

Max immediately felt sorry for trying to goad Emily into an argument. He was impressed that she hadn't fallen for it. Not one to hand out apologies easily, he told her, "Look, I'm sorry for being a jerk earlier." She smiled, and all was forgiven.

The rest of the evening was pure magic. They swapped holiday horror stories, and before he knew it, Max was telling Emily things he hadn't shared with anyone in a long time. He couldn't remember the last time he'd felt so accepted and understood.

THE WAY EMILY engages Max reflects her nature as an open-hearted person who is willing to speak and hear the truth. Her questions prompt Max to be reflective, and in return he softens and opens up to her. This might feel risky at first since it is quite new for him, but he takes the leap, and in doing so, he joins Emily in laying the first stone in a solid foundation for a potential relationship. Max and Emily are two very different people, but their conversation reveals a willingness to listen, learn and grow, possibly with each other.

Attracting Your Soulmate

Attracting your soulmate has nothing to do with your appearance, interests or lifestyle compatibility. It's about the person you are now, and your willingness to grow into the person you are destined to become. In this chapter, we're going to explore the nuts and bolts of preparing to be the partner you need to be for the soulmate who is out there—and ready to grow with you into a higher level of spiritual maturity.

Whether you're seeking to connect with a new soulmate or hoping to transform your existing relationship, it's important to remember that true romantic love is not all sweet and magical; in fact, it can involve much pain and sacrifice. Life might seem simpler if our partners were relationship employees and we could terminate their service if they didn't meet our needs. But embracing transformation through romantic love is about more than that. It is a way of being.

Yet, if we believe there is such a thing as true romantic love, and it involves sacrifice, how do we handle it when our needs and wants are not met by our partners, or if we and our partners are very different? I believe falling in love has a purpose. Romantic love is one of many vehicles to refine our human qualities in order to reconnect to our true nature. Needs propel us to create relationships, but they can also create tension and conflict. Growing a relationship organically requires certain tension between two partners to focus them into becoming the now—both being in the present moment together and merging into their joined future. A relationship filled with positive tension can push and challenge both partners to grow. This developmental process includes both love and suffering. Love without suffering is not true love, whereas suffering without love causes us to spiral downward through one lifetime after another.

There are spiritual and practical reasons why relationship employment exists. Growth cannot take place without a relationship, or without tension or conflict. Many of us have little interest in growing, and little interest in other people unless we want something from them.

Ironically, it is only in a conditional relationship that we can learn to love unconditionally. The human need for connection drives our interest in other people, with whom we might be able to work out our dysfunctional personalities. Through courageous self-reflection and compassion for each other, we can turn relationship employment into relationship-employment love, and eventually into the esoteric transformative experience of true romantic love.

But we must be ready for this. If we're not ready, we won't attract our soulmate, or won't recognize them when they come along. Instead we will continue to gravitate toward hollow, transactional relationships, or relationships that reinforce our wounds rather than healing them.

Giving and Receiving Love

A few years ago, I had the opportunity to construct a particular woman's energy chart. During my research into her life story, she mentioned a question that her grandmother had once asked her: Would she rather give love or receive it? She said that she would choose to give rather than receive because if she only received love, she would never experience what love is. Her definition of love was to give rather than to take.

Her choice reflected her idealistic heart. She did not fantasize about love. A Chinese woman, she married a Scottish man 26 years her senior. Because of the ethnic and age differences, her family was not initially supportive. She was a beautiful woman who would have had no trouble finding a man in her age group. In fact, she had a boyfriend around her age before she met her husband. Later, when I met her husband, I realized he was truly a remarkable man. Many experts say love cannot conquer differences in age, race, religion and other social categories that divide humanity. But they're talking about relationships, not love.

Many of us were raised in dysfunctional families in which we were not adequately cared for. In adult love relationships, we often want our partners to compensate for what we feel we missed in childhood (or to replicate dysfunctional childhood relationships in the hope of making them turn out better). Can receiving love without giving it back be called love? Most people would say no. But what about giving without receiving? Would it be a healthy long-term relationship if we play a mother or father role, taking care of our partners, and not receiving anything in return? If all we want is to selflessly serve without regard for our own needs, then we don't need a love relationship—we might as well go to India to volunteer at the Mother Teresa Foundation. It is perfectly fair to expect both parties in the relationship to give and take in an equitable exchange; otherwise, the long-term relationship won't work. But how does that work in a true romantic-love relationship that goes beyond conditions and transactions?

The Middle Way

Before becoming a spiritual leader, Gautama Buddha was a crown prince who revelled in sensory and materialistic pleasures. Yet his existential suffering drove him to seek salvation. Buddha moved from one extreme (pleasure and excess in the physical realm) to the other extreme (ascetic practice and deprivation, from which he almost died). At a critical point on his spiritual journey, he discovered what he believed to be the essence of life.

It's called "the Middle Way," or "the Middle Path."[1] The same principle has been discovered by sages in different cultures over and over throughout human history.

Here's an example. Let's say a person makes all the sacrifices in one relationship, but receives only pain and suffering in return. This causes them, in their next relationship, to seek a partner who will shower them with indulgences without any expectation of reciprocity. Like Buddha before he reached enlightenment, this person is stuck between two extremes. Ironically, when their mind is stuck in either extreme, there is no friction of needs, and they will not grow.

In fact, they will not grow until they are in a life situation where it is necessary to bring two opposing extremes into unity: to love and to be loved; to give and receive, at the same time. When they find their "middle way," they will heal the wounds created by the two extremes and move up to the next level of awareness. The Middle Way does not mean that sometimes you give and sometimes you take. The middle way comes into being when two opposing forces, to love and to be loved, synthesize into unity.

Surrendering to Love

Buddha's journey of the Middle Way demonstrates that growth and maturity require inner awareness stemming from direct experience—it is Buddha's personal experience that affirms the truth.

We are taught throughout our lives how to define love, according to our friends, parents, partners or spiritual teachers, but this is just a concept in our minds. There is a difference between learning the concept and experiencing the reality. It is an awakening experience when we embrace true love within, when an inner awareness shifts our state of consciousness. When we experience inner transformation, we label it using the concept of love we've learned from our culture.

Different forms of conflict and tension spur growth, the pre-condition to which is awareness. One form of tension is the struggle to decide whether to give love to a person who does not return those feelings. For most of us, our own metamorphosis requires our life to be changed by another person who shows us how true love involves suffering. Our being is changed by witnessing and being touched by this person's unconditional sacrifice. The following letter from a reader published in the *Vancouver Sun* newspaper many years ago exemplifies this.

Single friends have attended night school, joined art galleries and spend thousands of dollars on the ski slopes in hopes of finding a mate. Looking for love is hard work, and no one worked harder than me.

I met him at work. He was the kind of guy who brought a smile whenever he came to visit; he was good to my mom and great with my cat. He often made me cookies and he always made me laugh. Yet I never considered him marriage material. Inevitably I said those dreaded words, "Let's just be friends." He responded politely. "Okay, just friends."

Love was wearing a disguise when it came knocking at my door. I was looking for someone tall, athletic and Caucasian and with an unruly energy that would throw me about and mess up my head. I was wrong on both counts. You see, my friend was Chinese-Canadian. It was not that I had consciously excluded Asian men (or any other ethnic group for that matter) but I did not include them either. The feelings I experienced were unfamiliar too. I had never dreamed that love could be so uncomplicated, so much fun. The time spent with my friend was as calming as a Spanish Banks sunset and as easy as eating ice cream. There was often joy and rarely pain. This was new to me.

I remember the day I fell in love, or more accurately, the day I accepted his love into my life. It was late on a Friday night; we were busy filling the Christmas molds with chocolate to ready the truffles before the holiday season. As we shared entertaining stories of Christmas past, I was overcome by good feelings. It does not get better than this, I realized. I had in that moment, all I had ever wanted. The search was over, I had found love.

My friend became my lover and eventually my husband, but the root of our commitment has remained friendship. Sometimes we express our passion as lovers, and sometimes we plan our finances as partners, but we survive the daily grind as friends. It was a friend I needed when I lost my job and it was a friend I wanted when I found a better one. The pain and celebration of life is best shared with friends. Marrying your best friend, it turns out, can be very convenient.

Philosopher Erich Fromm once said, "Love is an act of faith." "To love," he continued "means to commit oneself without guarantee." In time, I recognized the truth in these words. Throughout our relationship I experienced love without conditions, without demands. I witnessed an act of faith as love grew in friendship and eventually in me. I have come to believe that love may not be difficult to find, but is sometimes difficult to see.

—*Vancouver Sun* reader Shauna M.

The author of this letter initially rejects her husband's romantic interest because he does not meet her compatibility checklist, which unconsciously excludes certain racial groups. This letter aptly illustrates one of the problems with the whole concept of the compatibility checklist.

Another problem with the compatibility checklist is that it sets us up for a transactional, conditional, needs-based relationship—relationship employment. But the whole point of Shauna's story is that her future husband wins her heart by demonstrating unconditional love, even after Shauna rejects him, no doubt causing him excruciating pain, and for a reason that's not only trivial, but one that he can do nothing about.

In spite of this, he brings his authentic self into the friendship with no demands. All these qualities create security and trust in Shauna's heart, which evokes closeness and intimacy later in her subjective reality. Because his feeling for her is congruent with his words, actions and desires, Shauna can tell he is not a fickle love consumer who will disappear from her life if he cannot get what he wants in return. She knows she can trust this man, which translates to a sense of safety and closeness.

If Shauna's husband were a love consumer without discipline of his emotions, her rejection would cause him to turn his back on her and look for another relationship right away. Most love consumers are relationship opportunists who cannot discipline their desires. He would not concentrate his time, resources and energy on Shauna if there were no return on his investment in the long run. He would not be patient and treat Shauna and her family with affection. If his love for Shauna were conditional, he would not commit to her without a guarantee, an act of faith with the understanding there may be no future with her. The result of practising the art of loving is the closeness and intimacy that Shauna shares with her husband, which comes as a result of Shauna being willing to open her heart.

Shauna's statement, "I remember the day I fell in love, or more accurately, the day I accepted his love into my life," can be understood as an "aha" moment. Shauna discovers more about herself and life through her friendship with this man. This discovery occurs because his simple act of being himself ignites her soul. With his unconditional love, she grows into a mature woman who can appreciate his finer human qualities. This intimacy cannot be forged by relationship skills taught in a self-help book or workshop. This intimacy is a kind of life wisdom embedded in self-sacrifice and unconditional sharing.

The underlying principle that made Shauna fall in love with her husband is similar to that of Wu Wei. This Taoist concept states that a desirable result is achieved without forcing something to happen. When two forces in a natural state align properly, something will occur organically. We cannot speed up the timing as change in humans has its own timing. When the timing is not there, we must accept it with grace. This is why Taoism appears passive.[2]

In other words, we can't make someone fall in love with us. If we use tricks to fabricate love, it will not be genuine. We may get our partner's body, yet we will not connect deeply with their soul. One of the characteristics of true romantic love is that we stumble into it. We cannot will it to happen. Shauna's story illustrates this point. Maturity has its own timing. Shauna must be able to see the wisdom of love for herself. But if her Chinese-Canadian friend, or someone else, were to tell her what love is supposed to be, her opportunity to learn and grow might be short-circuited.

None of us can learn life wisdom from a workshop or from reading this book. Wisdom requires self-reflection like Max's in the opening story. Max's inner state, as described in the story, illustrates that how he feels at the moment of self-reflection is an important part of his self-discovery journey. He describes his emotional state using similes to help himself consciously explore who he was in his past, who he is now and who he may be with Emily in the future.

Sometimes, truly authentic moral changes require a role model or example. In Shauna's case, exposure to her husband's life and personality help Shauna to change. She sees the finer qualities in her husband, such as the purity of his intentions. Shauna can feel that her friend's caring for her and her family is authentic. When Shauna's husband is in the present moment with no conditions attached, she opens up and connects with his energy. She feels he is trustworthy, and can relax around him.

That connection causes a gradual internal shift in her subjective reality.

For Shauna, the moment of falling in love is the result of the interplay of the subtle call-response of emotional attunement and connection. In the presence of the man who becomes her husband, Shauna feels no pressure from him. This excites her at a soul level. When he senses and sees that Shauna is enjoying being around him, this feeling resonates with his psyche. The vibrational energy flows back and forth between the two of them. This is a natural dynamism that any of us might experience if we are mindful during our interactions with one another.

There is another deep insight in this story that is not in Shauna's narrative, and that is her husband's perspective. When he first reveals his love to her, she rejects him. He faces an emotional dilemma: whether to continue to love Shauna, or to withdraw his love. How would you respond in this situation?

If it is true love, and we are at a later stage of development, our desire to see the other person happy, whether as his friend or his lover, will trump our desire to have our feelings returned. As mentioned, being in the now while in a meditative blissful state is easy. But when your feelings are not reciprocated, it is far more difficult. Despite the pain he must feel as a result of rejection, Shauna's friend sees that he has the opportunity to make her happy, which is what he wants most. If Shauna finds her true love elsewhere, he will let her go with serenity and dignity and let another man protect, cherish and honour her; that is the beauty and blessing of true romantic love.

Through the synthesis of love and pain in the present moment, his needs and desires are transformed. And the continuity of his feelings, even in the face of disappointment, reshapes Shauna's inner world. The changes within her in turn lead to changes outside of her, which allows the two of them as a couple to move into their shared future.

Closeness and Intimacy

Generally, it's agreed that closeness and intimacy are crucial to love. I see these concepts from a spiritual and existential perspective.

To me, both are the products of deep connection with oneself, with others and with life—what I call "relational love." This relational love can also lead to "spiritual love," which is a unity between one's heart/mind and the divine. Consequently, my ideas of closeness and intimacy go beyond the popular definition.

Closeness carries both physical and psychological meanings. Physically, we exist in a particular space and time. Because we use a physical body to identify ourselves and experience the world, we always feel separate from others.

The way to connect despite this physical separation is by working on our subjective reality by developing self-awareness. Psychological closeness means closing the emotional and psychological distance between our lover and us. However, it does not mean we lose the boundary between our partner and ourselves. If we feel lonely in a relationship, our higher self is reminding us that we have not found closeness and intimacy. Feelings of loneliness in a relationship typically mean we feel disconnected from others and from ourselves.

Developing closeness in a love relationship means creating safety and trust, which are the foundations of intimacy. In her book *Is It Love or Is It Addiction?,* psychologist Brenda Schaeffer outlines five characteristics of trust.[3]

1. ACCEPTANCE (unconditional positive regard): "I may not agree with you or like how you do or say things, but my caring for you is unwavering."

2. OPENNESS: "I will take risks with you and respectfully share who I am, what I feel, what I think, and what I do."

3. RELIABILITY: "You can count on my being there and my support for you will be strong."

4. CONGRUENCE: "I will work to make my words and actions match."

5. INTEGRITY: "I will honour my word to you. If I fail you, or me, I will own it and make my apology."

What Schaeffer describes are personality traits, which cannot be learned as skills, but can be cultivated through self-awareness, insight and wisdom. There are many self-help experts and spiritual gurus to teach us where and how to find love, some of which point us in the right direction and some of which don't. In Chapter 4, I suggested how you might distinguish between the two. Schaeffer is an insightful self-help expert and her book *Is It Love or Is It Addiction?* sets us on the right path: to find love, we must look within.

These lessons can have a metamorphic effect on your core being. You are trying to create love in a relationship, instead of simply letting love come to you in the relationship. Remember, you can create a relationship but you can only stumble into true love.

Yet closeness between two lovers does not mean there is also intimacy between them. In a state of closeness, two people still feel they are separate entities. In a state of intimacy, as I define it, two people merge into one. For example, some women talk about pregnancy as an intimate experience. But the mother and child are not merged, they're separate entities. This is not intimacy, it's closeness. The closest a man can come to this in life is sex, when his body is joined with that of his partner's. Sex and intimacy are synonymous in many people's love language, but the two lovers are not merged during the sex act; they're still separate entities, so this is also closeness rather than intimacy.

Intimacy and Sharing

While closeness may be a prerequisite for intimacy, intimacy goes beyond it. When intimacy is present, lovers feel a new being is emerging from the union. Falling in love narrows the distance between each lover's sense of a separate self. The extent to which partners can minimize the psychic distance between them reflects the quality of their romantic love.

Intimacy is built upon sharing. There are different degrees of sharing. The entry level is sharing interests, preferences, values, beliefs and outlooks on life. Two people feel like one as they share many aspects of each other's lives. They think, feel and act the same. Some people use the concept of the twin flame to describe this level of intimacy, which is merely similarity.

Deep sharing gives rise to a sense of merging two identities into one. Merging with another entity induces a sense of losing oneself temporarily, which can happen at different levels of consciousness. The kind of fusion I am going to discuss involves both structural changes in our souls and our state of consciousness; the change can be temporary or long-term.

Another level of intimacy is how the experience of falling in love changes you. You take on some of the same values and preferences as your beloved. You like and dislike the same things as your partner. For example, say you don't like wine, but after falling in love with your beloved, who drinks wine, you start to like it. This example is of course superficial, but the same holds true for adopting each other's values such as tolerance or generosity. If certain human qualities in your beloved inspire you to bring out similar qualities in yourself, there is a much deeper and more profound change in your sense of self, and this brings the two of you closer. The moment you realize you have changed because of this person, you have a deeper sense of intimacy. Your new self is the product of inspiration from your beloved, who breathes their life force into your consciousness.

A more advanced level of sharing and merging is non-verbal. Here, two people share their thoughts and feelings without speaking. It is in a wink, a smile or a lover's gaze that conveys understanding.

So how do we get to a higher level of intimacy? What does sharing look like on each of these levels? Spending an hour together on a first date or spending 20 years together in a marriage are both examples of sharing. What we share with our partner is time, but is it truly sharing? We share our body with our partner in bed... is this sharing too? A couple take out a mortgage and live in the same house... is this sharing? They create a new life, using the man's sperm and woman's egg... is this sharing? In one sense, of course, these are examples of sharing. Yet, material and physical sharing cannot remedy a lonely heart. What cures loneliness, angst and emptiness and creates real intimacy is the sharing of our subjective reality with our partners, connecting our heart/mind with our partner's heart/mind.

Deeper sharing, at the psychological, emotional and energetic levels, involves sharing our true feelings, both happy and painful, with our partners without defending our image and self-worth. When we share how we feel, what we think and why we experience life a certain way, we open up our perception and invite another person into our world. When this other can relate to our subjective consciousness, we expand our subjective space by creating an inter-subjective space. At the energetic level of our existence, two subjective spaces merge to create harmony. This makes us feel grounded and at home.

The most advanced level of sharing is the willingness to share in each other's suffering with empathic attunement and connection. A lover shares the beloved's suffering as if it were their own. In order to be part of the beloved's suffering, the lover sacrifices their own needs and desires to make the beloved feel that they are not alone in their pain.

Bridging the Gap to Intimacy

Marriage and long-term relationships have taken on a new importance in our society in the last 50 years. Couples who want to stay together forever and who want to find happiness and joy in the process of creating a shared reality must realize that marriage is not only a social arrangement to meet their individual needs. Rather, it must be a vehicle for personal growth.

The challenge is how to connect intimately despite being trapped inside our subjective reality. We may long to expose our thoughts and feelings to one another with trust and emotional safety. But that doesn't always happen. Because neither we nor our partners are free from dysfunctional personality traits, we inevitably have moments when our vulnerability is met with our partner's judgment or fear instead of compassion and understanding. These breaches of trust are painful and can drive a couple apart, unless both partners make a conscious effort to work on the underlying issues.

When experiencing relationship problems, many couples turn to relationship experts or therapists for help. Experts in the relationship field have developed several important concepts and tools to create the shared reality that can help clients remedy their relationship problems. While these can help some couples, for others they accomplish nothing, and at worst, they can pose new problems of their own.

Self-Disclosure and Listening

Sharing your thoughts, memories and feelings is the primary vehicle that many experts recommend to promote intimacy, but this doesn't always work. If talking about ourselves could cure our loneliness and existential fear and pain, chatty women and men would not feel lonely. Every day we talk so much, yet how often do we express our deeper feelings? We love to talk, perhaps because we are lonely. But if we devote every moment to talking, when do we listen? And how can we create closeness and intimacy if we're not listening?

We fear being judged, whether by ourselves or others. One defence against this is choosing not to examine ourselves so that we don't have to confront what we find. There are three reasons we might employ this defence mechanism.

1. A strong sense of guilt, shame and inadequacy. People who feel this way often ignore certain past emotional experiences. There is a powerful disconnection within their subjective consciousness. When a person tries and fails to achieve intimacy through self-disclosure, it may be owing to this type of self-censorship. When we try to tell our loved one how we are feeling and what we are thinking, we really only tell them what we want them to know. But how deeply can we share our perception with anyone if we cannot accept our own inadequacies?

2. Lack of awareness. Without awareness of how we create defence mechanisms, we are not aware of what motivates us to behave in certain ways. We know our heart is filled with emotions, but we don't know how to make sense of them, much less share them with others.

3. Misunderstanding ourselves. As an example, consider Scarlett O'Hara. The heroine of the classic 1939 film and Margaret Mitchell novel *Gone with the Wind*, Scarlett believes she is in love with her cousin Ashley. But at the end of the story, she realizes the man she truly loves is her husband, Rhett Butler. Like Scarlett, we may not intend to lie. Yet, we cannot truly share our experiences, emotions and our private self with others if we fundamentally misunderstand ourselves.

Active listening is one simple technique we can use to improve communication, which can lead to greater closeness and intimacy. It involves the following steps:

- Focusing on what the speaker is saying rather than mentally preparing a rebuttal.

- Using appropriate facial expression, body language and encouraging comments.

- Paraphrasing, clarifying and periodically summarizing what the other person has said.

- Avoiding interrupting; deferring judgment.

- Being candid, open and honest, and stating opinions in a respectful way.

For active listening to be most effective, the listener must have empathy. Therefore, the ability to actively listen depends on the listener's stage of development. Active listening is not difficult to learn in theory, but is difficult to put into practice. This is especially true of couples in emotional conflicts. In Max's story at the beginning of this chapter, the way Emily responds to his mood is an example of effective active listening that is grounded in empathy.

What Is Empathy?

Empathy is the ability to think and feel the same way as another person, which gives rise to feelings of caring and a desire to help. Because empathy has two dimensions, feeling and thinking, there are two ways to practise it. First, if we are emotionally sensitive, like small children or some animals, we can tune directly into another person's emotional state. That is, we can feel what they're feeling without intellectually understanding what is going on in their heart and mind. The purer our intention, the more easily we can tune into the other person's vibrational state via our physical senses.

The other way to practise empathy is by imagining what it is like to be that person in that moment by understanding their beliefs, thinking, experiences and desires. Basically, we put ourselves into the person's subjective world to think and feel the way they think and feel. This imaginative process is not only vital in developing our moral capacity, it can turn into a creative process when we engage with other people's emotional and energetic fields to create a novel interaction.

The effectiveness of active listening is based on our capacity to empathize, to put ourselves in the other person's inner world, to feel and think the way that person would, even if the story being told sounds crazy. To do this, we must find inner resources in our subjective space to honour this person's emotional experience without judgment.

But empathy begins with oneself. If we don't want to listen to our own negative inner voice, we can't really listen to what others have to say. Would we honestly want to understand another person if their stories only reminded us of our own repressed feelings of inadequacy? Connecting and sharing can only be deepened when we have empathy for our loved one, and we can only have empathy for our loved one when we have empathy for ourselves.

To invoke our capacity for empathy, we must put aside our own reality to become receptive and sensitive to the inner reality of the speaker. The more baggage and hang-ups we bring to an interaction, the more negatively we will interpret what we are hearing. Active listening should help us create a shared reality with the speaker. If our prejudices are getting in the way of understanding the speaker's reality, we can't practise active listening.

We also cannot develop active listening skills if we have no interest in another person's uniqueness, no curiosity about why they became the way they are. This lack of interest does not necessarily reflect self-centredness; more likely, it reflects a lack of curiosity about ourselves for fear of our own self-judgment. Most of us have difficulty developing active listening skills because we have no interest in knowing ourselves first. Consequently, many of us only know others on a need-to-know basis. That is, we only want to know others to the extent we can benefit from knowing them. The foundation of a lack of closeness and intimacy in relationships, then, is an inner feeling of disunity with ourselves and others. The primary cause of this is an inability to share our true authentic self with ourselves and others. As a result, we cannot actualize our divinity or our calling in life. This lack of heartfelt unity results in alienation, loneliness, emptiness, existential dread, neurosis and possibly addiction.

To escape these feelings, many of us seek happiness in a love relationship. In doing so, we indirectly stumble into an opportunity for spiritual transformation. If we transform our personality traits and desires in the relationship with our partner, the by-products we experience include closeness, intimacy and joy.

Feeling our Way toward Love

With so much mental static disturbing our clarity of mind, how can we ever hope to find and recognize our soulmates? Perhaps feelings should be our guide, rather than thoughts. The feeling we call love can be a confusing and unreliable lens to assess with whom we should have sex and create a relationship. What if that feeling disappears? Should we let go of the relationship? Even the great philosopher Bertrand Russell was perplexed by the experience of falling out of love. One day while riding his bicycle, he suddenly realized he did not love his wife.[4] With so much deep insight about human nature, Russell was still confused by his own feelings.

Feelings of love become even less reliable when we're trying to evaluate who we want most when there are two or three potential partners who all appear lovable to us, or if we become engaged in a love triangle. True romantic love evokes feelings, but those feelings, in and of themselves, are not true romantic love. True love is more than a feeling and more than relationship employment. This is where many people get confused and why many serious thinkers belittle romantic love.

All of us have an innate ability to receive energetic information from the universe or from within. When we train our psychic ability, we gain access to our own "hard drive" (the eighth consciousness/soul) and improve our capacity to connect to the universe, which is sort of a spiritual version of the World Wide Web. Thus, there are two sources of energetic information: our higher selves and our connection to the universe. Training our psychic ability has a profound effect on this.

I am most interested in clairsentience, which is the ability to attune to the emotional vibrational frequency of another person and to feel their emotions or physical sickness as if they were our own. It is a more refined form of emotional connection and attunement, which is the ultimate source of true romantic love. We are all psychics; we are born with empathic capacity (with the exception of people with certain mental-health issues, such as psychopathy or narcissistic personality disorder, in which the ability to empathize is impaired or missing). Without empathy, we could not love. If you have the capacity to love others, I would assert that means you also have psychic abilities.

Clairsentience has deep implication in relationships, love, morality and spirituality. Perhaps our greatest spiritual sages, such as Jesus, Mohammad, Buddha and Confucius, had unusual clairsentient capacities. Because they were able to feel others' pain, their compassion motivated them to devote their lives to alleviating suffering.

We have the capacity to attune and connect with other people's emotions. Some of us even have the capacity to attune and connect with others' energetic fields the way an AM/FM radio tuner captures signals. With such a capacity, we can create a shared reality with others emotionally and energetically. In this way, attunement is a creative act.

Psychic ability manifested as emotional attunement and connection can be expressed in different ways depending on which level of reality we're trying to access. For example, a small child can intuitively attune to an adult's pain. Think of an old man who has just lost his wife of 50 years, and a four-year-old girl who climbs onto his lap and puts her head against his heart to comfort him. This empathic attunement is a manifestation of her innate psychic ability.

Unfortunately, over the course of our lives these abilities become dormant. There are two reasons for this. One is the overwhelming influence of Western culture. Because it values intellectual capacities over other capacities, Western cultural conditioning has taught us to repress our psychic abilities. But psychic abilities have a use-it-or-lose-it nature, so if we're not using them, we're—you guessed it—losing them. The second reason is that, with the exception of a few highly gifted psychics, these abilities naturally recede as we mature. We can, however, reclaim them by practising energetic techniques and exercises such as meditation, yoga, qigong and breath work.

We can also experience emotional connection and attunement in a shared socio-psychological reality. For example, say a group of longtime friends spends a weekend together. At one point, they are at a restaurant when a waiter says something ordinary, such as, "May I take your order?" The friends all look at each other and burst out laughing, not because the waiter has said anything funny but because they're remembering and sharing some inside joke about a similar situation in the past. They are experiencing emotional connection and attunement in a social situation.

Attuning yourself empathically means listening with your heart and soul. But what does this mean in less poetic, more pragmatic terms—that our hearts and souls have some mysterious auditory capacity? Probably not. To me, listening with your heart and soul means using your energetic ability to attune to another person's energetic state. This ability hinges on the three mental capacities of intention, attention and concentration.

Our ability to listen with our hearts and souls is a measure of how pure our motives are and how quiet and focused our minds are. There are two types of attunement and connection: empathy and call-response. Both begin with the person quieting their mind enough to tune into the other person's emotional vibration. They must be sufficiently aware of their own body's vibrational state to tune into the other person's vibrational state.

Call-Response Attunement

A call-response experience is a tool to create a shared reality, which may give rise to a deep bonding experience. In call-response activity, one person responds to their partner's vibrational signals either consciously or unconsciously. The psyche picks up the partner's vibrational field and the energy is filtered through the body to create a sensation. This sensation directs your intention, or your intention directs your sensation, to respond in a certain way. If your energy flow is in sync with your partner's, the call-response between you is effortless and spontaneous, and you can create a novel and unrepeatable experience with your partner.

A good example is theatrical improvisational training. All the improvisers are in the present moment. They respond to the other actors spontaneously. The actors do not know beforehand what they will do or say.

During sex, when two partners seem to be responding to each other on a completely non-verbal level, that too is an example. In fact, most shared activities can turn into call-response experiences, even if they're adversarial in nature. In the classic Chinese military treatise from the fifth century BC, *The Art of War,* Sun Tzu points out that to know your enemy, you need to know yourself, and to know yourself, you need to know your enemy.[5] (In colloquial English, we might say "it takes one to know one.") In war, army commanders are familiar with the histories of their counterparts, right down to intimate details of each other's habits and lifestyles. They delve deep into each other's psyches to experience their rival's reality as if it is their own. Ironically, they may come to know each other so well that they develop deep mutual respect and almost regret what they must do to the other on the battlefield.

A high level of call-response attunement is intuitively sensing each other's feelings, thoughts and intentions. At this point, those in attunement can anticipate each other's actions in a way others not engaged in the relationship cannot. It can occur in any kind of competitive activity, such as chess, poker, tennis, or team sports. Those who compete at an elite level must study and know their opponents so intimately that they form a kind of mutual bond, a bond they can only form with others who are functioning at the same level. Someone at our own level brings out the best in us and pushes us. That is the essence of call-response attunement. This is why, under normal circumstances, we attract others who are at our own stage of development or self-awareness.

The Dance of True Romantic Love
I like to compare love to dancing, another activity that can create intimacy using call-response attunement and connection. On the dance floor, two dancers swirl around each other. If both know the steps, play their respective roles, and are in the moment, they can make a difficult skill look effortless. Quite often, amateur

dancers, even though they know the steps, cannot elevate to the next level because their minds are not present with their partners. Or they cannot elevate to the next level until they find the right partner. But what does this mean?

We identify good dancers not only by their skills but by their ability to communicate and create synergy. In freestyle partner dancing, the woman does not know the intention of the man's lead and the man does not know how the woman will respond. To dance as a unit, they have to raise their awareness of each other by synchronizing their bodily movement, breathing, skill and intention in perfect time with the rhythm of the music. The rhythm of the tune unconsciously regulates the breathing of two dancing partners, indirectly unifying their attention in the present moment. The emotional union of the two dancers through their movements must be in tune with the emotional dimension of the music. Two highly trained dancers' minds become one in this emotionally hypnotic state.

Instead of two separate dancers on the dance floor, they become a unit, losing themselves in the moment together when they reach the perfect synchronization in tune with the music and their breathing. A lot of high-level dancers experience a moment on the dance floor that they claim is better than orgasm. This form of intimacy is beyond words and concepts. Dance partners often become romantically involved because, through dancing, they form a temporary erotic bond.

Many dances, such as salsa, are highly sensuous and bring out the erotic dimension between two dancers. When two dancers become one, the unity of a new consciousness takes up the entirety of the dance floor. When you look at their facial expressions and sense their vibrational state (spirit), it appears that the pair has found a new level of confidence. They don't feel small when they experience this special (erotic) unity. This is why I don't advise people to find their mates in the dance hall! You might confuse your dancing experience with falling in love.

Spiritual Oneness and Intimacy

Most of us don't dance professionally and don't compete at an elite level. Yet almost all of us have social relationships with others, including romantic and sexual relationships. Have you ever experienced intimacy and closeness in a heartfelt relationship with another human being or during sex, a state in which you lose yourself together with your partners?

Intimacy in the situations described is the expression of two or more independent consciousnesses merged into unity, which is in essence no different from the merged souls of two lovers when they share their bodies or innermost selves. This intimacy is similar to a mystic experiencing union with God. Although the expression is different, the underlying principles and experiences are the same.

Many spiritual teachers use the concept of oneness to describe a transcendental state. The concept of oneness presupposes the merging of the consciousness of the subject and the object into one. The object can be the entire cosmos or another human being or activities, or anything other than "I." In other words, oneness means the merging of two consciousnesses into a unity that transcends space, time and bodily state.

The Spiritual Practice of True Romantic Love

It is possible to experience unity alone or in a partnership. We saw the former in the example of St. John of the Cross, the Christian mystic who had a mystical experience with the divine. But the state of unity I describe in this book does not have any religious overtones. We can choose to experience our being as is, without labelling it according to organized religion.

With the unity of two minds, a truly deep fusion of two consciousnesses may expand the feeling of humanity within these two individuals and give them a glimpse of the existence of something other than their physical, psychological and energetic dimensions. This intimate altered-state experience can have a powerful and profound effect on how we see ourselves and our lives, just as a near-death experience can change the course of a person's life. If our personality is at a more advanced stage of development, this non-differentiated state of unity with even one other person can help us feel bonded with our fellow human beings at a much deeper level.

We are here to learn how to love and to shine our light. We choose our life partner because with them we glimpse a new possible self. Togetherness brings out the divine and makes us want to share our life's journey with this other soul.

If you are currently seeking a relationship, remember this as you search for someone with whom to share your earthly life. If you are in a relationship in which you no longer feel in touch with the divine, ask what you can do to transform your relationship with yourself and your own soul. Whatever your situation, always remember, true romantic love is there for all of us. We need only choose the path of learning and growing. We need only prepare ourselves to be ready when it comes our way. And, likely when we least expect it, we will stumble and fall—into true romantic love.

FURTHER CONSIDERATION

· What do you think it means to be ready to be the partner you need to be to attract your soulmate? What do you need to do in your life to get yourself ready?

· What qualities made you choose your partner?

· What do you think it means to find your own "middle way"? For example, what does it mean to you to love and be loved? What does the term "give and take" mean to you? How do you go about balancing your needs and your partner's needs?

- How would you define the word "closeness"? How would you define the word "intimacy"? What, if any, difference do you perceive between the two?

- How can a shared activity between you and your partner create a deeper shared reality? Give an example from your own relationship.

- Why do you think it's important to understand yourself? Why do you think this is so difficult? What bearing do you think this has on understanding others, or being understood by others?

- How do you try to connect with yourself, others and life? Have you ever experienced a sense of profound unity with others and life? If so, what did it feel like to you?

NINE

Everlasting Romantic Love

WHAT DOES THE word "romantic" mean to you? Does it mean looking out on the ocean from the balcony of a five-star tropical resort with your loved one? Or a candlelit dinner for two at an elegant restaurant? Or making love on a white-sand beach? Or does it mean something a little more easily accessible, such as watching children play in a park, or holding hands while eating cotton candy at a fairground on a fall night?

There is a difference between a romantic moment and romantic love. Before we end, I wish to explore this distinction. This will help us understand why true romantic love is everlasting, why we can only stumble into it, and how it can spiritually transform two lovers.

Most people have an idea that the word "romantic" can only describe a state or a mood induced by the external environment.

But like love itself, romance does not exist independently from human qualities. Romance does not originate outside of us, but within our romantic personality. What is a romantic personality? Love is romantic because two lovers are idealistic, novel, unique, and creative. These human qualities make love both romantic and unforgettable.

Idealism

In my view, romanticism is closely linked to idealism. The idealism embedded in true romantic love cannot be captured in a grand theory put forward by philosophers who use abstract concepts to depict love in a way to which few people can relate. True romantic love is more than a relationship, more than something that can be studied by researchers in labs and learned from reading self-help books and attending workshops.

The spark of true romantic love begins with a feeling that resonates with the lover's higher ideals. Feelings generated by our imagination are fleeting, but if our soul is touched, it will bring forth a special image or thought-form that embodies our ideal values and cannot be so easily dismissed. Romantic lovers feel something beautiful in the depth of their souls, even if they cannot articulate it. The power of this mysterious ideal makes lovers want to move into a perfect state of consciousness with the person who has evoked it. This idealism manifests in different forms.

The Merriam-Webster dictionary defines idealism as "the attitude of a person who believes that it is possible to live according to very high standards of behaviour and honesty."[1] Romanticism, meanwhile, is described as "the quality or state of being impractical or unrealistic."[2] It is strongly associated with "the imagination and emotions," according to the dictionary definition.

As different as the two ideas may seem, there is a lot of overlap between them. Idealism is often considered "impractical or unrealistic" and is associated with "the imagination and emotions," while romanticism can be considered as referring to certain "standards of behaviour and honesty." Both are driven by strong passions and conviction.

Yet in our culture, idealism is generally held in much higher regard than romanticism. Consider two young women, one fictional, the other real. The first is Juliet, the heroine of Shakespeare's tragedy *Romeo and Juliet*, who was willing to die for love. Romeo was her ideal lover, and she had the idealistic notion that she should be able to marry him even though their families were mortal enemies. She believed true love could or should conquer all.

The second woman is activist Malala Yousafzai. Malala became internationally known when she was shot in the head by Taliban terrorists for defending girls' right to education. Though she almost didn't survive the attack, today she has recovered and continues to fight for her ideals.

Both women are romantic figures who put themselves in harm's way for ideals they fervently believed in. Yet while Malala is revered for her courage in pursuing an ideal she is willing to die for, Juliet, who was willing to die for her ideals of love, is regarded by some as irrational, her behaviour considered absurd, unjustifiable, groundless and even shameful. It seems we don't believe romantic love is worthy of the ultimate sacrifice, but if the cause is justice, freedom, equality or other human rights, it is worthy. We can be romantic and idealistic in one situation, but not the other.

But true romanticism, no matter what its inspiration, always embodies our highest ideals. And our highest ideals are always somewhat romantic in that they usually spring from imagination and emotions. They represent high standards of behaviour, and are often considered by those lacking imagination and high standards of their own to be impractical and unrealistic.

But why should this be the case? Romanticism and idealism can both be considered vehicles for personal growth. When we fall in love, there is one less selfish, me-first person in the world. With the blessing of true romantic love, we are rich in our hearts and bursting with compassion. We want to share this inner bounty with everyone, including strangers. Falling in love brings out qualities such as caring, consideration, sweetness and warmth that you didn't know you had in such abundance. Thus, we set out to inspire other people with hope, to help others believe in themselves and to offer them solace when they are in pain.

True romantic love does not immunize us from a broken heart. Yet, because it is true romantic love, the laughing, the crying, the pain, the sharing and the mistakes help guide us toward maturity. When we look back on painful experiences, we realize that they were simply the price we had to pay to grow into better, wiser and more feeling versions of our selves.

There are other practical benefits to being both idealistic and romantic. If one is idealistic and mature, the chance of falling in phantom romantic love and experiencing a string of relationships that cause serious pain is lessened because our ideals are a form of belief in higher values. If idealists are congruent, their personality structure personifies the ideal, which becomes an objective standard and expectation that they use to evaluate themselves and potential love interests. With such high expectations, not many people can match their ideals. The problem with modern romantic love is that many of us have no such ideal. Romantic love has been reduced to a fast-food-type sensory and socio-psychological experience.

Apart from idealism, three other things underpin true romantic love: novelty, uniqueness and creativity.

Novelty

Novelty is not about newness and excitement, but freshness. The source of novelty in romantic love is the freshness of our minds, which creates a romantic spark the moment we fall in love. But this feeling rarely lasts. Why do we so often lose the feeling of novelty once a relationship solidifies?

It might be because we enter into relationship employment, in which we see our beloved as a supplier whose purpose is to meet our needs. We then go forth in our mundane, predictable and repetitive life and grow bored. We begin to look elsewhere for excitement.

Another reason is that many of us stop striving toward growth in our relationships. Although our beloved is the same person, they are changing every day at the micro level. If our minds keep growing together with the changes in our beloved, we will always see something fresh about our beloved.

Think of it this way. Suppose that, in your spare time, you studied astronomy. As time goes by you use increasingly more powerful telescopes to observe a celestial object, for instance the moon. All your life you have been observing the same object, yet you never tire of it because each year you use a better telescope and see more. Every year, a familiar object becomes new. And every time you see it in a new way, you learn something new about it, which increases your understanding and appreciation for it.

Consider what Chan Buddhism calls "the beginner's mind." With the beginner's mind, every time we look at a long-time partner, we feel like we are meeting them for the first time. Life is always novel. If we fail to see its freshness, the failure is with our own mind.

Uniqueness

Uniqueness means that the experience is not repeatable but always original. Two elements make true romantic love unique: the essence of the beloved and space/time. In 2014, during a round of significant hostilities between Israel and Palestine, a wedding between a Jewish Israeli bride and an Arab

Palestinian groom took place. They were cursed and threatened by extremists on both sides. If they had married for relationship employment, they would have had plenty of people to choose from and would likely not have made such a contentious choice. But when we fall in love with one person, there is only one option.

Life is about joy and suffering; true romantic love makes both states better. There is a difference between sharing your life with just anyone and sharing it with someone who deeply connects with you. When we experience something good, our joy is increased if we can share our good fortune with someone we love. When life turns unpleasant, we find the strength to endure it when we have a special person beside us.

With this person, we are willing to be seen as naked in our heart and soul. This is the only person to whom we can pour out our dreams, pains, fears and secrets. Only this person attunes to our soul. This is the person to whom we call out when we are in distress and who responds with that magical love that calms and mesmerizes us. Few people in our life truly understand us, yet this person understands who we are and assumes a new dimension of intimacy with us. Our soul has found a resting place and sanctuary, and we finally know what it means to be home.

The second dimension of uniqueness in romance is space/time. Our romantic personality must engage with our beloved's romantic personality to create a romantic moment. Every love story has its own unique setting in space and time. But while some love stories take place against a backdrop of history, as in the case of the Jewish bride and her Arab groom, it does not take a monumental historical event to make a love experience unique, memorable and impactful. Consider two people who happen to meet at the one moment they're in a particular place they've never been before and never will be again. The uniqueness of meeting ignites the romantic spark.

Creativity

There are two major components to creativity: conceiving an idea, and turning it into reality. But there is a difference between regular creativity and romantic creativity. Romantic creativity is about more than conceiving and actualizing an idea. Romantic creativity is about creating a sense of surprise and delight in the beloved's heart.

This element of surprise is only possible when a lover knows their beloved well and employs intention, attention and concentration to achieve the desired effect. The lover's *intention* must be to surprise the beloved, to disrupt their way of experiencing the world or thinking about themselves. The lover devotes their *attention* to acknowledging and uplifting the positive qualities of the beloved. Then the lover must *concentrate* on transforming the idea into reality. The more difficult this transformation, the more concentration required.

Here is an example. Let's say your partner loves music and loves to sing. You know that he wrote a song when he was 16 and dedicated it to his mother. To honour this memory, and despite the fact that you hate to sing in public, you secretly take guitar lessons. Using the same guitar on which he first played the song for his mother, you play it for him at a family gathering on his birthday. He is deeply touched and filled with good feelings because your gift embodies the purity of the intention, attention and concentration for him in your mind and heart. This is another example of a call-response moment.

The Nature of Love

Just as the sun will always rise and set, life will always follow the same patterns. It's not just the passage of time, but the repetition of a habitual cycle that causes lovers to lose their romantic passion. When this happens, they stop seeing changes in their lives and themselves. However, if they strive to remain as mindful of life and each other as they were on the day they met, they will find idealism, novelty, uniqueness and creativity in every sunrise and sunset, with every lovemaking occasion or any time they do anything else in this world. It's only when we allow our minds to become stuck that life and love become boring.

True romantic love is not a volcanic eruption in the lovers' consciousness, or an outpouring of hot lava from their hearts. After all the hot sex and passion subsides, what is left is reality. True romantic love is grounded in life, which can be romantic but can also be mundane, habitual and practical. Yet if a relationship is built around true romantic love, life can be continuously wondrous and surprising.

Once the roots of two romantic souls are intricately intertwined, differences that might at one time have seemed insurmountable, such as race, socio-economic background, age, or language, can no longer set them apart. The real test of true romantic love is whether the bonding of two souls can transcend the waning of sexual passion over time. Can the strength of their romantic love overcome major life obstacles blocking their union? Can the power of their love give them the will to transcend their personality differences, addictions and the pressure of their mundane lives? Can the resilience in their romantic love enable them to forge a common identity without losing their individuality in the process? Most importantly, do the two lovers have the moral character to be physically and emotionally faithful for the rest of their lives?

True love transforms our human qualities. The journey and power of true romantic love begins with the consciousness of being and moves into the consciousness of becoming. When two people fall in love, they grow together in a life they create. Their transformation along the way into new and better people is what makes romantic love so beautiful.

True romantic love is romantic because the idealism embedded in romanticism is grounded and can survive the pressures and challenges of life. It is the frustration and friction between two lovers that brings out their tenderness, patience, and understanding. It is their flaws that help them learn to forgive and accept. It is their shared experience of learning to accept each other's flaws and differences that cements their romantic love.

If the connection between two lovers is true romantic love, they can find idealism, novelty, uniqueness and creativity even amid the boredom, lethargy, and doldrums of life. The heart-pounding breathlessness, awkwardness and enthusiasm they felt while falling in love can become purity, simplicity and warmth. As the river of time flows forward, these qualities evolve into serene silence, intimacy and gentleness, even into the twilight years of a couple's romantic journey.

The romantic dimension of love does not change, but the way the lovers express it can. Simply put, what changes is not the love they have for each other, but the way in which they experience and express their love. With pure intention, attention and concentration, every little moment in life brings out the greatest romantic joy between them.

Love is when you have no interest in an activity like whale-watching, but you smile when you see how much your partner enjoys watching whales swim wild and free in the ocean.

Love is when you lose your breast to cancer and your partner kisses the surgical scar and says you will always be the most beautiful person in the world to them.

Love is when your mother dies, and your partner holds you while you cry for three hours.

Love is when you are angry because your boss has blamed you for something you didn't do, and your partner listens while you rant.

Love is when the family is getting bigger and your partner suddenly loses their appetite for pricey Starbucks coffee and takes on a second, part-time job.

Love is going on a trip and forgetting your sneakers, and your partner walks with you for hours in a Burmese night market so you can find the right size of shoe.

Love is when your partner cuts your hair for you for 40 years because you've never found anyone who cuts it as well as they do.

Love is when both you and your partner are hungry and there is only one piece of bread, and each of you offers it to the other.

Love is when your lover sees how much pain you carry inside your heart that you cannot share with anyone else and suffers quietly with you.

If you feel anything when reading these lines, I hope it's recognition that these are the moments that make true love romantic. Notice that the romantic qualities have nothing to do with candlelit dinners or expensive gifts, or the kinds of shared activities so many relationship experts recommend. Instead, these are the ordinary gestures that become romantic when your beloved brings them to you with their heart and soul. A romantic moment is not difficult or expensive to create if we bring our human qualities into every present moment.

Love Never Dies

The final important quality of true romantic love is that it is everlasting. Once romantic lovers are transformed by love, they are no longer the same. True romantic love transforms our moral selves, and actualizes our authentic selves.

True romantic love is a story. It takes place at a specific place, time and setting with a specific set of rules. Both lovers bring their unique life circumstances, experiences, expectations and personalities into the present moment as they create a script that is theirs, and only theirs. The conflicts and challenges they face create a romantic spark that bonds the souls of the two beyond their respective psychological selves. Their story is about the transformation of their character, human qualities and their fate. Consequently, it is natural for two souls to never forget the experience or the person with whom they shared it.

That said, the ending will depend on the story itself. In life, there are no guarantees of happiness. As previously mentioned, Aristotle said that a story must have three phases, a beginning, a middle and an end. At the end, the protagonist learns the life lesson they need to learn and the person is transformed because of it. This is as true of a true romantic love story as of any other story in life.

But even if a true romantic love relationship ends because one partner dies, or because one or both partners agree that the relationship is at an end, the love itself does not end. True romantic love is everlasting because its existence does not depend on the relationship. The qualities that emerge within true romantic love continue to live beyond it. From a reincarnation worldview, these refined qualities embody the true romantic love we experience in our current life and carry forward to the next Earth life as we wait to meet our soulmate once again and pick up where we left off. This is why true romantic love is everlasting.

In the end, the most important thing to remember is this:

Hope is love and love is hope.
We will all return home, to love, together.
No soul is left behind.

FURTHER CONSIDERATION

· Before you read this book, what did the word "romantic" mean to you? Has the book changed your thoughts on this? If so, how?

· How would you differentiate romantic love from a romantic moment?

· Do you believe true love can last forever? If so, why? If not, why not?

- How do you (or would you) keep your love fresh with your partner?

- Life is uncertain. How can the power of true romantic love help you face that uncertainty in ways that relationship employment and phantom romantic love cannot?

- What can you do to build a new identity with your partner while continually ensuring that you do not lose your uniqueness and individuality?

- What personality traits do the two of you need to be sexually and emotionally faithful for the rest of your lives and to overcome your differences of personality, desires and needs?

Epilogue

One child, one teacher, one book and
one pen can change the world.
— MALALA YOUSAFZAI

WHILE RESEARCHING THE subjects of fate, true romantic love and the soulmate connection, I found a common pattern among my research participants' life journeys. In their teens, they tended to feel isolated and lonely, due to a lack of self-awareness. In their twenties they felt disconnected and disappointed in their love lives, due to a misunderstanding of the nature of love and relationship. In their thirties, they were burned out on suffering and depression after a string of broken hearts, then finally looked to therapy and spirituality for guidance in their forties or fifties. By then, not only were their psyches feeling broken, their bodies were often suffering serious ailments brought about by stress and emotional disturbance.

Too often, we don't understand why it is that in order to love others we must first love ourselves. In youth, many of us have

no awareness that all relationships, including romantic relationships, have a moral component. The truth is that the quality of
our love relationships reflects the level of our moral maturity
because we always bring our morality and other human qualities
to bear in creating a romantic relationship. To be a responsible,
loving partner, we must have the maturity to know what we
really want out of life, love, sex and relationships. With maturity
comes the ability to reflect on the experiences that have made us
who we are and learn from our mistakes. If we have little idea of
why we have turned out the way we have without embracing any
sense of accountability, we will continue to defer responsibility
to others, resigning ourselves to an inability to change and grow.

Some of my research participants truly discovered themselves and attained great wisdom through therapy after suffering
setbacks. Yet not everyone recovers from a broken heart or love
addiction. Many people continue to struggle with tremendous
personal agony throughout their lives, entrenched in depression,
addictions and fear as they mistake toxic relationships for romantic love. This takes an enormous toll on their social resources as
well as their physical and mental health.

I have come to see our misunderstanding of the nature
and purpose of romantic love not only as an individual challenge, but as an epidemic social issue that disrupts harmony
and drains tremendous public resources. Damaged mental and
emotional health affects our GDP by sapping productivity, and
raises the collective cost of our insurance, medical, law enforce-
ment, correction facilities and legal services. But even this pales
in comparison to the human cost. It's easy to measure a loss of
productivity in the economy, but we cannot measure human suffering in dollars and cents.

It's hard to create peace and harmony within communities if large numbers of people are suffering from mental health
issues caused by childhood traumas, addiction caused by low

self-esteem, and broken hearts caused by toxic relationships. But society cannot change unless the human qualities we bring into our relationships and communities change for the better. Many social problems can be traced back to an earlier point in an individual's life in which they were deprived of love and positive relationships in childhood or adulthood.

I could not help but ask myself whether we might be lifted out of this tragic situation if we were given tools at an early age to understand ourselves, and to know the difference between a wholesome relationship and relationship addiction. As with physical ailments, prevention is a much better approach to combating the problem than any form of treatment could be. How much happier, healthier and more productive might society be if we were all instilled with a sense of our own innate worthiness of love in childhood?

The primary place we learn about love and relationships is at home with our families of origin. Yet many of us grew up in dysfunctional families with unhealthy relationship role models, leading us to develop emotional handicaps. Having said that, even being born into a loving family is no guarantee that we will grow up self-aware in our relationships. Many of us have no idea we have an addictive relationship style until our hearts have been broken many times.

If we cannot learn these critical life lessons at home, I would hope that we might at least have the chance to learn them at school. Although our education system provides sex education to young people, the most essential aspects of romantic life are not taught: what love is, how to love, why we love, why we became the person we are now, and how to understand ourselves and our partners in the midst of creating a relationship. There is no self-love and self-awareness education, and minimal instruction on mental and emotional health. To reduce the loneliness, emptiness and despair that are the source of relationship addiction, young people need to know how to cultivate positive human qualities in themselves and create healthy relationships with themselves and others. A morality-based curriculum of self-awareness and healthy relationship skills could enable the next generation to avoid developing life-damaging relationship habits, or at least spur them to seek counselling earlier in adulthood, before many years of toxic energy are invested in dysfunctional, addictive patterns.

The thesis of romantic love in this book cannot be fully learned in the classroom setting, because the power of true romantic love can only be experienced in the presence of one's beloved. However, when we are properly taught self-awareness and relationship principles, the training itself can enable a young mind to mature faster, and prepare the individual for loving, functional relationships later on.

What's more, I believe that a program like this could also increase the harmony in our communities. Imagine how bullying at school and online might be reduced if young people were taught about emotional intelligence, or trained in energy exercises such as qigong, yoga or meditation. Just as these practices can foster self-awareness and resilience in adults, they can also refine young people's physical, energetic and emotional sensitivity. Communication and the capacity for understanding between teens and their parents would also improve if teens were taught self-awareness techniques that might enable them to better understand their own and their parent's emotions, thought patterns and reasons for behaving as they do. Perhaps we can even reduce the instances of unwanted pregnancy, addiction and suicide.

Years ago, I was speaking with a participant in my research project about a number of concerns I found in her energy chart, when she suddenly closed her eyes and began sobbing. She said that she had just realized that she had been re-enacting her mother's dysfunctional behaviour, which had hurt her greatly as a young person. Seeing her own ignorance and blind spots for the first time, she told me that she wished she'd had more self-knowledge in her teens, which might have led her to accept her mother and avoid unconsciously perpetuating her mistakes.

Another research participant who was addicted to sex and dysfunctional relationships had broken up with his girlfriend for reasons he could not make sense of. He knew he had to get out of the relationship, he said, because it was "too good to be true." This man was unaware that he was actually breaking up with his own good fortune to prove to himself an unconscious belief that he was incapable of loving others or being loved. Responding to a request from his ex-girlfriend, this man wrote a long letter to the hypothetical new boyfriend she would be with in her next relationship. As he read the entire letter to me under a moonlit sky, I knew that he was describing the man he truly wanted to be, and the love and relationship he desperately wanted to experience but did not know he was capable of. I told him that he, like all of us, was born with the capacity to love another soul in the way he described in his letter, but would probably need to undergo therapy to break his addictive patterns before he could be ready for the true romantic love that was his birthright.

Society cannot afford to continue to wait for its members to seek emotional help in their thirties, forties or fifties, when the resources needed to recover are greater than in youth, and the likelihood of recovery so much lower. My greatest wish for this book is that it should initiate a social movement to raise awareness of the importance of teaching the younger generation how to develop self-awareness and an understanding of love, morality and relationships.

If you, too, can see the benefit of educating young people on these critical life skills and insights, I encourage you to join me in campaigning for self-awareness education in our schools, specifically self-awareness in the context of relationships, moral integrity and mental health. This new love and self-awareness curriculum need not be based on any particular worldview, since love and self-awareness are universal humanistic values independent of religion or ideology.

The first way in which you can help is to sign the online petition at geraldsze.com to tell our local and federal governments that you want to see a change in the high school curriculum. And while you are there, I invite you to send a message to me through the website to share your ideas about how we might work together to realize this vision.

Second, I urge you to organize a local chapter of this community to bring our movement to your local school board. I truly believe that together we can create a grassroots movement to urge lawmakers, school trustees and educators to include love-based, self-awareness education in at the high school level.

Third, you can make a statement about your values by giving a copy of this book to socially conscious organizations and to your friends and families, and by asking them to pass it on to their friends and families in turn.

By passionately campaigning in this way for love and self-awareness education, we can make a lasting difference that ripples out beyond our immediate communities to positively affect the lives of people around the world. Please join us in our efforts to lift up humanity, to ease our collective suffering and to help us all to live in greater love, hope and happiness.

NOTES

CHAPTER 1

1   John A. Brentlinger, ed., *The Symposium of Plato*, trans.
Suzy Q. Groden (Amherst: University of Massachusetts Press, 1970).

2   Theodore M. Ludwig, *The Sacred Paths: Understanding the Religions of the World*, Fourth Edition (Upper Saddle River, NJ: Pearson, 2005).

3   Gerard Encausse, "Reincarnation and Religion," Rose Cross Order website, rosicrucian-order.com/revista_reenc.htm.

4   Pew Research Center, "'Nones' on the Rise," October 9, 2012 http://www.pewforum.org/2012/10/09/nones-on-the-rise/.

5   Michael Newton, *Journey of Souls: Case Studies of Life Between Lives* (Woodbury, MN: Llewellyn Publications, 1994), p. 88.

6   *Wikipedia*, s.v. "Yogachara," last modified February 6, 2017, https:// en.wikipedia.org/wiki/Yogachara.

7   Gerald Sze, *Changing Fate Through Reincarnation: How the Fusion of Responsibility, Freedom, Karma and the Meaning of Life Can Set You Free* (Minneapolis: Two Harbors Press, 2012).

CHAPTER 2

1   See "Ayahuasca: Vine of the Soul." Written and directed by Richard Meech (Toronto: Meech Grant Productions Ltd., 2010), DVD, 48 minutes. vineofthesoul.com.

2   Erich Fromm, *The Art of Loving* (New York: HarperCollins, 1956).

3   1 Corinthians 13: 4–8 (New Revised Standard Version).

4   Barbara Ann Brennan, *Hands Of Light: A Guide to Healing Through the Human Energy Field* (New York: Bantam Books, 1987).

5   Joseph Campbell, *The Hero with a Thousand Faces* (San Francisco: New World Library, 1949).

6   Bruce K. Alexander, *The Globalisation of Addiction: A Study in Poverty of the Spirit* (Oxford: Oxford University Press, 2008).

CHAPTER 3

1   Helen Fisher, *Why We Love: The Nature and Chemistry of Romantic Love* (New York: Henry Holt and Company, 2005).

2   Thomas S. Kuhn, *The Structure of Scientific Revolutions* (Chicago: The University of Chicago Press, 1962).

3   Dorothy Tennov, *Love and Limerence: The Experience of Being in Love* (New York: Stein and Day Publishers, 1979)

4   Tennov, *Love and Limerence*, p. 23–24.

5   Tennov, *Love and Limerence*, p. 22.

6   Tennov, *Love and Limerence*, p. 119–20.

7   Radical Reading's. "The Road Less Traveled: Love, the myth of romantic love," *Radical Reading's* (blog). radicalreadings.wordpress.com/2011/06/10/ the-road-less-traveled-love-the-myth-of-romantic-love/.

8   M. Scott Peck, *The Road Less Traveled: A New Psychology of Love, Traditional Values and Spiritual Growth*, Timeless Edition (New York: Touchstone, 2003).

9   Erich Fromm, *The Art of Loving* (New York: HarperCollins, 1956).

10 *Wikipedia*, s.v. "Relationship obsessive-compulsive disorder," last modified February 6, 2017, https://en.wikipedia.org/wiki/ Relationship_obsessive-compulsive_disorder.

11 *Wikipedia*, s.v. "Crime of Passion," last modified February 8, 2017, https://en.wikipedia.org/wiki/Crime_of_passion

12 Ann Landers, "Infatuation Or Love? A World Of Difference," *Chicago Tribune*, April 18, 1998, http://articles.chicagotribune.com/1998-04-18/ news/9804180019_1_dear-ann-landers-column-piano

13 Newton, *Journey of Souls*, pp. 260–61.

14 *Wikipedia*, s.v. "Yogachara," last modified February 6, 2017, https:// en.wikipedia.org/wiki/Yogachara.

15 Barbara Murphy. *Quantum Possibilities* (blog) quantumpossibilities.
    biz/clairs.htm.

CHAPTER 4

1 Fanny Moser, *Spuk: Irrglaube oder Wahrglaube?* Foreword by
   C.G. Jung. (Zurich: Gyr, 1950), p. 10.
2 Jane Loevinger, *Ego Development: Conceptions and Theories* (San
   Francisco: Jossey-Bass, 1976).
3 See Jean Piaget, *The Moral Judgment of the Child* (London: Trench,
   Trubner and Co., 1932) and Lawrence Kohlberg, *Philosophy of
   Moral Development: Moral Stages and the Idea of Justice* (New York:
   Harper & Row, 1981).
4 Relationship Dynamo, "The Psychology of Relationships: What
   is Symbiosis?" *Psych Relations* (blog). psychrelations.blogspot.
   ca/2011/02/psychology-of-relationships-what-is.html.

Chapter 5

1 Kieran Kavanaugh and Otilio Rodriguez, trans., *The Collected Works
   of Saint John of the Cross*, Revised Edition (Washington, DC: ICS
   Publications, 1991), p. 470.
2 *Wikipedia*, s.v. "Taoist sexual practices," last modified February 6,
   2017, https:// en.wikipedia.org/wiki/Taoist_sexual_practices.
3 *Wikipedia*, s.v. "Tantra," last modified February 6, 2017,
   https://en.wikipedia.org/wiki/Tantra.
4 Barbara De Angelis, *Are You The One for Me?: Knowing Who's Right
   and Avoiding Who's Wrong* (New York: Dell Publishing, 1992).
5 Robert M. Pirsig, *Zen and The Art of Motorcycle Maintenance*
   (New York: William Morrow and Company, 1974).
6 Aristotle, *Nicomachean Ethics*, 8.3.1156b6–12.

CHAPTER 6

1 Darren Star, Ollie Levy and Michael Patrick King, "La Douleur
   Exquise!", *Sex and The City*, season 2, episode 12, directed by Allison
   Anders, aired August 22, 1999 (New York: HBO Home Video, 2001),
   DVD.
2 *Wikipedia*, s.v. "Loevinger's Stages of Ego Development," last
   modified February 10, 2017, https://en.wikipedia.org/wiki/
   Loevinger's_stages_of_ego_development

3 Friedrich Nietzsche, *Twilight of the Idols* (Indianapolis: Hackett Publishing Company, 1997)
4 Abraham Maslow, *Motivation and Personality* (London: Pearson, 1954).
5 Zhena Muzyka, *Life by the Cup: Inspiration for a Purpose-Filled Life* (New York: Atria Books, 2014).

CHAPTER 8
1 *Wikipedia*, s.v. "Dhammacakkappavattana Sutta," last modified February 6, 2017, https://en.wikipedia.org/wiki/Dhammacakkappavattana_Sutta.
2 R.L. Wing, *The Tao of Power* (New York: Doubleday, 1986).
3 Brenda Schaeffer, *Is It Love or Is It Addiction?* (Center City, MN: Hazelden, 2009), p. 163.
4 *Wikipedia*, s.v. "Bertrand Russell," last modified February 6, 2017, https://en.wikipedia.org/wiki/Bertrand_Russell.
5 *Wikipedia*, s.v. "Sun Tzu," last modified February 6, 2017, https://en.wikipedia.org/wiki/Sun_Tzu.

CHAPTER 9
1 *Merriam-Webster OnLine*, s.v. "idealism," https://merriam-webster.com/dictionary/idealism
2 *Merriam-Webster OnLine*, s.v. "romanticism," https://merriam-webster.com/dictionary/romanticism

PERMISSIONS

GRATEFUL ACKNOWLEDGMENT IS made to the following sources for permission to reprint from previously published material.

Quotations (pp. 53–56) from *Love and Limerence* by Dorothy Tennov used by permission from Rowan & Littlefield.

Quotation (p. 59) from the column of Ann Landers by permission Esther P. Lederer Trust and Creators Syndicate, Inc.

Quotation (p. 62) from *Journey of Souls: Case Studies of Life Between Lives* by Dr. Michael Newton © 2002 Llewellyn Worldwide, Ltd. 2143 Wooddale Drive, Woodbury, MN 55125. All rights reserved, used by permission.

Quotation (pp. 190–91) from *Is It Love or Is It Addiction?* by Dr. Brenda Schaeffer (Center City, MN: Hazelden, 2009). Used by permission.

GERALD SZE is an award-winning author and existential spiritual philosopher. His explorations have included Eastern and Western philosophy, divination and comparative religion, as well as an immersion in Buddhism. Sze published his first book, *Changing Fate Through Reincarnation*, in 2012. He lives in Vancouver, Canada.